The Atlantic Slave Trade

Lucent Library of Black History

Other titles in this series:

The Atlantic Slave Trade

Lucent Library of Black History

Don Nardo

LUCENT BOOKS

A part of Gale, Cengage Learning

GALE
CENGAGE Learning

Detroit • New York • San Francisco • New Haven, Conn • Waterville, Maine • London

GALE
CENGAGE Learning

LIBRARY OF CONGRESS CATALOGING-IN-PUBLICATION DATA

Nardo, Don, 1947–
  The Atlantic slave trade / by Don Nardo.
      p. cm. — (Lucent library of black history)
  Includes bibliographical references and index.
  ISBN-13: 978-1-4205-0007-3 (hardcover)
  1. Slave trade—Africa—Juvenile literature. 2. Slave trade—Europe—Juvenile literature.
  3. Slave trade—America—Juvenile literature. I. Title.
  HT1322.N37 2008
  306.3'62—dc22

                                                              2007022999

ISBN-10: 1-4205-0007-4

Printed in the United States of America
2 3 4 5 6 7 12 11 10 09 08

Contents

Foreword

It has been more than 500 years since Africans were first brought to the New World in shackles, and over 140 years since slavery was formally abolished in the United States. Over 50 years have passed since the fallacy of "separate but equal" was obliterated in the American courts, and some 40 years since the watershed Civil Rights Act of 1965 guaranteed the rights and liberties of all Americans, especially those of color. Over time, these changes have become celebrated landmarks in American history. In the twenty-first century, African American men and women are politicians, judges, diplomats, professors, deans, doctors, artists, athletes, business owners, and homeowners. For many, the scars of the past have melted away in the opportunities that have been found in contemporary society. Observers such as Peter N. Kirsanow, who sits on the U.S. Commission of Civil Rights, point to these accomplishments and conclude, "The growing black middle class may be viewed as proof that most of the civil rights battles have been won."

In spite of these legal victories, however, prejudice and inequality have persisted in American society. In 2003 African Americans comprised just 12 percent of the nation's population, yet accounted for 44 percent of its prison inmates and 24 percent of its poor. Racially motivated hate crimes continue to appear on the pages of major newspapers in many American cities. Furthermore, many African Americans still experience either overt or muted racism in their daily lives. A 1996 study undertaken by Professor Nancy Krieger of the Harvard School of Public Health, for example, found that 80 percent of the African American participants reported having experienced racial discrimination in one or more settings, including at work or school, applying for housing and medical care, from the police or in the courts, and on the street or in a public setting.

It is for these reasons that many believe the struggle for racial equality and justice is far from over. These episodes of discrimination threaten to shatter the illusion that America has completely overcome its racist past, causing many black Americans to become increasingly frustrated and confused. Scholar and writer Ellis Cose has described this splintered state in the following way: "I have done everything I was supposed to do. I have stayed out of trouble with the law, gone to the right schools, and worked myself nearly to death. What more do they want? Why in God's name won't they accept me as a full human being?" For Cose and others, the struggle for equality and justice has yet to be fully achieved.

In many subtle yet important ways the traumatic experiences of slavery and segregation continue to inform the way race is discussed and experienced in the twenty-first century. Indeed, it is possible that America will always grapple with the fallout from its distressing past. Ulric Haynes, dean of the Hofstra University School of Business has said, "Perhaps race will always matter, given the historical circumstances under which we came to this country." But studying this past and understanding how it contributes to present-day dialogues about race and history in America is a critical component of contemporary education. To this end, the Lucent Library of Black History offers a thorough look at the experiences that have shaped the black community and the American people as a whole. Annotated bibliographies provide readers with ideas for further research, while fully documented primary and secondary source quotations enhance the text. Each book in the series explores a different episode of black history; together they provide students with a wealth of information as well as launching points for further study and discussion.

Considering the African Perspective

The Atlantic (or transatlantic) slave trade lasted nearly four centuries—from the late 1400s to the mid-1800s. During that period, at least 10 million and possibly as many as 20 million black men, women, and children were taken from their homelands in Africa and shipped across the ocean to become slaves on plantations and farms in North, South, and Central America and the Caribbean islands. These rough estimates of slave numbers do not take into account those who died, or were murdered outright, on the dreadful voyages across the ocean. They also do not begin to tell the story of how entire societies in western Africa were disrupted, corrupted, and eventually had their populations depleted by the awful human trade.

Indeed, the total effect of the Atlantic slave trade in misery and death was so great as to constitute one of the largest human tragedies in history. In Kiswahili, the most widely spoken tongue in sub-Saharan Africa, the slave trade has come to be called the Maafa. This term translates literally as "disaster" or "terrible happening." But in the twentieth century African historians came to translate it more often as "holocaust," an English word meaning a great assault on or slaughter of human beings. Accordingly, the Atlantic slave trade is often referred to as the "African American holocaust" or the "holocaust of enslavement."

Whatever one chooses to call it, the Atlantic slave trade was a huge and horrendous event that colors the history of hundreds of millions of people alive today. As stated on the Web site of the Sankofa Project (a U.S. organization dedicated to highlighting African American heritage):

> The Transatlantic Slave Trade is probably the most horrendous and traumatic event [ever to occur] in the Western hemisphere. To the descendants of Africans now residing in North America, South America, and the Caribbean, it is definitely the most significant event in our history. . . . [It] turned portions of the African continent into chaos, empires rising and falling based on their quota of slaves. The brutalities and degradation these victims existed under was daily and never-ending. And the legacy would continue to their children and descendants for generations to come. This was the Transatlantic Slave Trade, an event which destroyed peoples and whole cultures; an event which would destabilize a continent, changing it forever; an event which would enrich Europe, create empires, and build America.[1]

European vs. African Views of the Slave Trade

The idea that many successful modern nations, including the United States, were built partly on the labors of enslaved millions is still not widely understood or acknowledged in said nations. In general, historians point out, Americans and Europeans do recognize that slavery and the slave trade did happen. And all agree that these were morally wrong and unfortunate events and practices.

However, the manner in which most white Americans and Europeans view the slave trade often differs from the way the descendants of the African slaves see it. "The collective memory of enslavement for Africans is very different from that of Europeans and their descendants," states the nonprofit research organization African Holocaust.

> To many white people, slavery and colonialism are just a distant memory of a short period in history. In Britain and the United States, many whites believe that slavery did not last particularly long, its benefits went only to a small proportion

of white people, and the evils of slavery are overshadowed by the role played by British abolitionists. To people of African descent though, the memory is a very different one. Slavery and colonialism affect everyday lives and evoke poignant and immediate memories of suffering, brutality, and terror. The memories are of Britain and the USA achieving their economic prosperity on the back of African enslavement. . . . Many people believe that the racism that grew out of African enslavement is the reason for today's racial inequalities. And it is these different interpretations of the effects of slavery that resulted in many groups celebrating Columbus, while so many others condemned him.[2]

Thus, many modern white people assume that the slave trade and its many evils are long since over and therefore not particularly relevant to today's world. Yet many black Africans feel that they continue to live with prejudice, economic hardship, and other negative aftereffects of slavery and the slave trade every day. For them, the slave trade—the Maafa—is more than a mere historical footnote. It is an integral part of their heritage and identity, whether they like it or not.

African Participation in the Trade

One crucial difference between the white American-European perspective and the black African perspective is the way each views the participation of West Africans in the trade. Throughout the almost four centuries in which Africans were shipped across the ocean, African chiefs and other local leaders aided the white slave traders. The fact is that slavery was practiced in most sub-Saharan black societies. And Africans regularly sold some of their own slaves to the Portuguese, English, French, Dutch, and other whites who landed on West African shores seeking cheap labor. "Many [African] rulers knowingly went to war with their neighbors, killing millions and destroying entire communities in order to capture fellow Africans for sale," admits noted African American scholar Kwaku Person-Lynn. "Maintaining power, expanding the economy, greed, and expansionist ambitions were the prime motivating factors."[3]

Like some white historians, Person-Lynn thinks that the direct participation of Africans in the trade is an unpleasant reality that

African leaders sell slaves to a white slave trader in this 1826
illustration.

must be accepted as a fact of life. "There is no way anyone can
defend or justify African involvement in the slave trade," he says,
"other than [to] acknowledge that it is one of many historical facts
that must be faced."[4] According to this view, many blacks share
the historical blame for the trade and its horrors along with the
white traders who regularly exploited Africa.

In contrast, other scholars point out that African involvement
in the slave trade was not a completely voluntary act. First, they
say, some African leaders felt compelled to take part out of fear. In
some cases, whites, who had more advanced weaponry than most
Africans, threatened to make war on those African tribes that
refused to help them enslave other Africans. "It is important to

look at the choices of Africans during critical periods of the slave trade," says African American historian Anne C. Bailey:

> The slave business, promoted as it was by persistent European and American forces as well as African middlemen, had largely marginalized all other types of economic activity in [western Africa]. Within this context [and] under substantial pressure for slaves from [white] slave traders, Africans had few choices [regarding ways to maintain their economic prosperity].[5]

A wide array of books, films, and museums recall the horrors of slavery and the lessons learned from this terrible chapter in American history.

Also, some scholars point out, it was not entire tribes or nations that decided local policy about capturing and selling slaves. Rather, a few greedy leaders made such decisions and forced their peoples to take part. "Here, it is morally and factually important to make a distinction between collaborators *among* the people and the people themselves," writes African American scholar Maulana Karenga: "Every people faced with conquest, oppression, and destruction has had collaborators among them, but it is factually inaccurate and morally wrong and repulsive to indict a whole people for a holocaust which was imposed on them and was aided by collaborators."[6]

Remembering Those Who Suffered

In spite of differing opinions about African involvement in the slave trade and the historical significance of the trade itself, all modern observers agree on one point: This horrible chapter in the human saga must not be forgotten. It must be taught in schools, and books, articles, museums, documentary films, and Internet Web sites must continue to examine and memorialize it. As Bailey puts it, slavery and its evils should be kept in the public consciousness "as a means of remembering so that we do not repeat the crimes of the past." In the end, she says, "may this tragic period of history be remembered for the purpose of honoring those who did not survive it and addressing the problems and the challenges faced by those who did."[7]

Chapter One

The Rise of the Slave Trade

The Atlantic slave trade was one of the most profitable commercial ventures in history. At the same time, it was one of the most violent, inhumane, and downright murderous episodes in the long and eventful human saga. "Through the four centuries of the trade," one expert observer writes,

> horror was compounded upon horror for the Africans who were herded to the rivers and shores and put aboard the slave ships. The black man caught up in the man traffic knew nothing but despair and misery. The swirl of this commerce reached into every corner and crevice of his continent and the curse was visited upon every tribe in some manner or another.[8]

The exact size and scope of the slave trafficking that crisscrossed the Atlantic from the 1400s to the 1800s is unknown. The most often-quoted modern figure is 10 to 12 million slaves transported across the Atlantic Ocean, many (perhaps as many as a third) of whom died on the way. Other estimates range as high as 20 and even 40 million. The reason that no precise figures will ever be known is that no exact records were kept. True, individual ship captains knew how many slaves they carried on specific voyages and in specific seasons. But hundreds and eventually thousands of ships from many different countries took part in the trade over the course of generations, and no one thought it necessary to keep an overall count for the sake of posterity.

As for which countries led the transatlantic slave trade, modern historians have managed to piece together estimates of the major participants. Portugal, one of the earliest European players in slave traffic, was responsible for a whopping 46 percent of the slaves transported from Africa to the Americas. Britain was second, with about 28 percent of the trade; then came France, with 13 percent; the Netherlands and Spain, with roughly 4.5 percent each; British North America (later the United States), with 2.5 percent; and Denmark, with somewhat less than 1 percent.

The Muslim Slave Network

It is natural to ask how these nations became involved in trafficking human beings on such a huge scale. After all, slavery was not

A medieval lord watches his serfs plant vines and pick grapes.

Black Slaves in Portugal

———————————————— ■ ————————————————

The first African blacks brought to Portugal in the mid-1400s became either household servants or laborers on sugar plantations. A Portuguese royal courtier of that era, Gomez de Azurara, described some of these slaves in his book *Chronicle of the Discovery and Conquest of Guinea*.

> They never more tried to flee [after we captured them], but rather in time forgot all about their own country. They were very loyal and obedient servants, without malice. . . . After they began to use clothing, they were for the most part very fond of display, so that they took great delight in robes of showy colors, and such was their love of finery that they picked up the rags that fell from the coats of other people of the country and sewed them on their own crude garments.

Quoted in Ulrich B. Phillips, *American Negro Slavery*. Whitefish, MT: Kessenger, 2004, p. 1.

very common in Europe in medieval times (the period lasting from about A.D. 500 to 1500 or 1600). For cheap labor, especially agricultural workers, most well-to-do people in that era relied on serfs. Mainly tenant farmers, serfs were technically free but also closely dependent on big landowners for a place to live, food to eat, and military and legal protection. As long as these highly dependent workers existed in large numbers in Europe, there was little need for slaves.

However, the slave-owning traditions of ancient times, which had culminated in the huge-scale slavery institution of ancient Rome, were not dead. In the early medieval centuries they remained alive and viable in various areas on Europe's periphery, most notably among Arabs and other Muslims in the Middle East and North Africa. In the seventh and eighth centuries, following the rise of Islam in Arabia, Muslim armies spread outward and created an enormous empire. It stretched from what is now Iran and Iraq in the east, across North Africa, to southern Spain in the west. The Muslims maintained prosperous cities with impressive political and legal systems and centers of learning. And well-to-do members of society supported their comfortable lifestyles partly through exploitation of slave labor.

For the most part, these slaves came from sub-Saharan Africa. Islamic law forbade Muslims from enslaving each other, but Muslim merchants found a ready source of black African captives in the lands lying just beyond the southern reaches of the Sahara. Some of these captives worked in homes and fields in the Muslim lands bordering the southern Mediterranean Sea. Other black slaves were forced to convert to Islam and serve in Muslim armies. Historians estimate that a total of nearly 10 million sub-Saharan Africans were forced into slavery in Muslim societies from the seventh through eighteenth centuries. Thus, a large and sophisticated trans-Saharan slave network existed throughout medieval times and beyond.

Arab slave traders bring slaves to market. Wealthy Muslims relied on slave labor to maintain their comfortable lifestyles.

Genoese and Portuguese Sugar Plantations

The transatlantic slave trade was, at least at the outset, an outgrowth of this slave trafficking network long maintained by Muslim merchants. But over time Europeans began tapping into the sub-Saharan slave markets. In the 1300s the Genoese, the inhabitants of the Italian kingdom of Genoa, began to see the economic potential of sugar plantations. Arab growers had been running such plantations in Egypt, Syria, and other areas of the Middle East for some three centuries. And the Genoese now copied the Arab model, including importing black slaves from Africa. By the early 1400s, Genoese growers and traders had begun to buy African slaves through the trans-Saharan network to work on plantations on Cyprus and other Mediterranean islands.

Justifying the Slave Trade

—■—

At first, overt racism played little part in the acquisition of blacks in the Atlantic slave trade. But over time many whites tried to justify their immoral and brutal buying and selling of other human beings by insisting that blacks were racially, mentally, and morally inferior to whites and therefore it was all right to enslave them. Most Europeans came to accept some variation of the argument as expressed by a nineteenth-century French nobleman named Arthur de Gobineau:

> The negroid [black] variety [of human] is the lowest [of the races], and stands at the foot of the ladder. The animal shape that appears in the shape of the pelvis is stamped on the negro from birth, and foreshadows his destiny. His intellect will always move within a very narrow circle. . . . We come now to the white peoples. These are gifted with [a great deal of] intelligence, [and history] shows us that all civilizations derive from the white race, that none can exist without its help, and that a society is great and brilliant only so far as it preserves the blood of the noble group that created it.

Arthur de Gobineau, *The Inequality of Human Races*. Trans. Adrian Collins. New York: Putnam, 1915, pp. 205–10.

These plantations were financially very successful, so it was not long before the chief European trade rivals of the Genoese, the Portuguese, sought to set up their own sugar plantations. Like the Arabs and Genoese before them, the Portuguese saw that growing sugar was a complex, expensive proposition. Indeed, "sugar was a distinctive crop," historian Stuart B. Schwartz points out:

> It called not only for good land and a particular climate, but also for particularly heavy capital investment [outlay of money] in buildings and equipment and a large labor force dedicated to continual and heavy activity during certain periods of the year. Europeans engaged in few activities more complex than sugar production in the early modern period.[9]

In the 1440s and 1450s eager Portuguese investors and growers created large sugar plantations on the Cape Verde Islands, Madeira Islands, and Canary Islands, all lying off Africa's northwestern coast. Initially, they imported white European workers. Condemned prisoners, indentured servants, and orphans were among those who labored on these plantations. But over time the owners found it increasingly difficult to find the large numbers of workers they needed in Europe, which had fixed supplies of cheap labor. The solution to this problem was to follow the Arab and Genoese lead by bringing in black African slave laborers.

The Portuguese found that importing black African slaves was not difficult. Adventurous Portuguese ship captains had recently been sailing south to explore Africa's western coast. Negotiating directly with local chieftains for slaves proved easier than tapping into the more time-consuming trans-Saharan network to the north. In 1444 Portuguese vessels carried some 240 black slaves to Lisbon, and many of these laborers were then transported to plantations in the Madeira and Canary islands. Shortly before 1500 Portuguese merchants and growers set up a thriving sugarcane industry on Sao Thomé, an island lying a few miles off the western African coast, and took advantage of black African slave markets to supply the fields with cheap labor.

Spanish Labor Needs in the Americas

The lucrative Sao Thomé plantation became the chief model for the European sugar plantations that sprang up in the recently discovered Americas in the early 1500s. At first, the Portuguese and

19

Leaders of Portugal and Spain negotiate the Treaty of Tordesillas, which gave Portugal control of western Africa and Brazil and gave Spain control of Central America and the Caribbean.

Spanish dominated both colonization and the slave trade in the so-called New World. The 1494 Treaty of Tordesillas between the two nations gave Portugal virtual control of the western African region and Brazil, while Spain acquired control of Central America and the Caribbean region.

The Spanish were the first to set up sugar plantations in the Americas, with an operation on the island of Hispaniola, east of Cuba, by 1502. Such outposts became known as colonies of "exploitation" or "tropical dependencies." The growers concentrated on turning out large quantities of cash crops—not only sugarcane, but also spices and cotton. In order to make a decent profit, all these crops required large numbers of inexpensive workers.

At first, the Spanish plantations did not do as well as their owners had expected. First, Spanish investors and governors increasingly shifted their resources into looking for gold and other valuables in Mexico. Second, Spanish growers at first exploited the existing native populations for cheap labor rather than importing large numbers of black Africans. This approach proved unproductive because the Native American workers quickly died out or became too few to turn a profit. On Hispaniola, for example, the Spanish had worked to death or simply outright murdered 80 percent of the island's original 250,000 inhabitants by about 1515. By 1650 all these natives were gone.

To replace those who had been exterminated, the Spanish turned to two sources—cheap white European laborers and black slaves from Africa. The white laborers—including convicts, war prisoners, orphans, and indentured servants—had been exploited for generations in Europe and elsewhere. But it had become more and more expensive to import them from Europe. Also, increasing social pressures demanded a shift from exploitation of white labor to exploitation of black labor, especially from the early 1600s on. As Minnesota State University scholar Johannes Postma explains, ultimately black "Africans became the preferred labor force," in part because of ingrained cultural values:

> Although Europeans often exploited their [white] workers harshly, treated their social inferiors with disdain, and punished offenders brutally, including torture and cruel executions, they increasingly refrained from reducing them to slavery. Only outsiders, people who were different [especially racially so] and had no roots in a community, were made chattel slaves [those completely owned, legally speaking, by their masters]. In that sense, Europeans acted like Muslims, who enslaved outsiders, or "infidels," but protected fellow Muslims from that fate. [10]

Thus, over time the Spanish increased their importation of black African slaves, which increased the profitability of their exploitation colonies. Throughout the 1500s and well into the 1600s, they bought African slaves from Portuguese traders, who still controlled most of the West African markets. After 1640, when Spain and Portugal became enemies, the Spanish turned to the Dutch, French, and eventually the English for supplies of black slaves.

The Portuguese, English, and Others

In the same years that the Spanish plantations were experiencing mixed success, the Portuguese created an extremely profitable plantation system in Brazil. The Brazilian plantations used black slaves early on, following the successful Sao Thomé model. Some attempts were made to exploit the local Indian populations, but as happened with the Spanish, these efforts proved mostly fruitless. The first black African captives crossed the Atlantic to Brazil in 1538, and by 1600 almost all the workers on the Brazilian plantations were black. Black slaves were also imported to work in Portuguese gold mines in central Brazil and on coffee plantations in the southern part of the country.

Black slaves work on a plantation in Brazil. Slave labor helped make these plantations profitable.

Meanwhile, other Europeans began competing with the Spanish and Portuguese. In 1627 the English opened their first sugar plantation on the island of Barbados. By 1643 only sixteen years later, they had imported more than 6,000 African blacks to the colony. By 1667 more than 40,000 blacks lived and worked on Barbados, almost twice the number of white colonists.

English, Dutch, and other European merchants also established successful exploitation colonies on the Caribbean islands of Jamaica, St. Croix, and Guadeloupe. Particularly profitable was the French Caribbean colony of St. Domingue. When French planters took control of the island from Spain in the late 1600s, they immediately began exploiting black slaves (some of whom had been imported earlier by the Spanish) as a workforce. By the late 1700s the colony supported some 28,000 whites of French ancestry, a roughly similar number of mulattos (people of mixed race), and a staggering 455,000 black slaves.

The Triangular Trade

The Caribbean, Brazilian, and other American colonies that came to exploit large numbers of black African slaves also took advantage of a very profitable commercial network that developed in the 1500s and 1600s in the Atlantic region. It became known as the triangular trade because it featured three primary legs or profit-producing steps. The first leg of the triangle consisted of the export of goods from Europe to Africa. In deals struck with African chieftains who owned large numbers of slaves, European merchants swapped these goods, including liquor, fabrics, and gunpowder, for black slaves.

The second leg of the Atlantic triangular trade was the sale of the slaves in the Americas. This sale turned a profit for the slave traders. It also allowed the buyers—the plantation owners—to turn their own subsequent profits because the slaves they purchased were inexpensive to feed and clothe. The slaves were also cheap enough to make it viable to regularly replace agricultural slaves who died of overwork. At the same time, household slaves, who had less backbreaking jobs, could be bred, producing two, three, or more slaves for each one bought from a slave trader.

The third and final leg of the triangular trade was the sale of goods produced by the slaves in American colonies to markets in

Europe. Sugar, cotton, tobacco, molasses, rum, spices, and other goods turned out by American plantations and farms flowed into Europe, turning still another profit for enterprising traders. With this profit, merchants bought the necessary trade goods to use in Africa, in the first leg of the next three-way trading cycle.

Such large-scale mercantile operations particularly benefited big investors. As a rule, only wealthy traders—those who could afford to own fleets of ships—could afford to take an occasional serious loss and still manage to keep putting money into new slaving ventures. "Ownership of the ships that traveled [the] triangular route [across the Atlantic and back] proved the most effective hedge against financial risk," scholars Madeleine Burnside and Rosemarie Robotham explain:

> Profits and losses could be spread among several ships, and the owners could control the choice of captains for each voyage. Indeed, the nature of the whole transatlantic enterprise suited the wealthy over the small investor, and many

A Slave Trade Contract

At first, the Spanish had no access to the African coast, so they had to buy slaves from Portuguese and Dutch traders. Here is part of a surviving contract made in 1667 between Spanish growers and Dutch slave traders.

The individuals mentioned [above] have agreed with each other on the following contract. The respective directors of the [Dutch] West India Company shall dispatch from time to time an adequate number of ships and cargoes to the coast of Africa and there purchase a total of 4,000 deliverable [acceptable] slaves . . . and deliver these during the current year, 1667, and before the end of December 1668 at the island of Curaçao to the agents of the [Spaniards mentioned above]. When these 4,000 Negroes have been handed over . . . they will be paid for as stipulated below.

Quoted in Johannes Postma, *The Dutch in the Atlantic Slave Trade, 1600–1815.* New York: Cambridge University Press, 1990, p. 350.

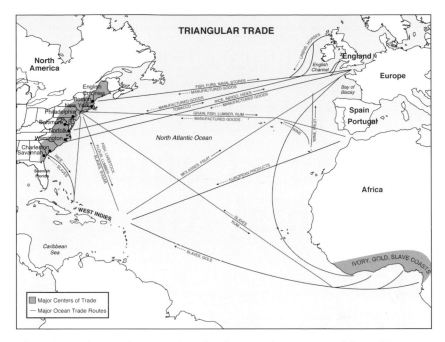

The triangular trade route involved natural resources shipped from the colonies to England, manufactured goods shipped from England to the colonies and Africa, and slaves from Africa shipped back to the colonies.

of the smaller speculators in the trade saw their fortunes destroyed by a single slaving venture that failed. Those who could afford to sponsor a significant number of slaving voyages, however, could expect their fortunes to grow.[11]

All the European nations that took part in the Atlantic slave trade exploited the triangular trade to one degree or another. But England became especially adept at it. This was partly because the English developed a highly diversified range of colonies. In addition to their exploitation colonies in the tropics, they established settlement colonies on the eastern coast of North America. (A settlement colony is one in which people set up towns and farms in an attempt to transfer a small piece of the mother country to a foreign locale.) At first, these colonies, including Virginia, the Carolinas, and Georgia, needed and used few black slaves. But over time the need increased, and the institution of slavery became entrenched in colonial America and the infant United States.

Chapter Two

Slavery Comes to Colonial America

English North America, the area along the eastern seaboard that later became the infant United States, was the last region of the Americas to begin importing black African slaves. Indeed, at first there was no significant need for black slaves in England's North American colonies. First, these colonies were situated too far north to support large-scale sugar plantations, which required long, hot summers and heavy rainfall to thrive. Second, as settlement colonies, the British outposts were small in size and scope, so there was initially a minimal amount of menial labor to be done and no need for large numbers of cheap laborers. Third, and most important, most of the English colonists came to America to exercise their religious and/or political freedoms rather than to seek economic wealth. As a result, the early colonists fully expected to run their farms and do other necessary work to maintain their communities themselves.

Eventually the English-speaking colonists began raising certain large-scale cash crops, especially tobacco. At some point, it became clear that more workers, ideally inexpensive ones, were needed to ensure a reasonable profit. Several different approaches were open to the colonists to fill this need. They could import white indentured servants from England, the Netherlands, and elsewhere in Europe; they could exploit Native Americans by capturing them and forcing them to work; or they could import black Africans in the manner of the Spanish and Portuguese exploitation colonies to the south.

The colonists experimented with all three of these approaches. And in time they found that the most viable was to import more black slaves. Still, the number of African slaves in colonial America remained relatively small for a couple of generations. Only in the 1700s did importation of blacks increase substantially. And when this happened, the manner in which blacks were treated, both socially and legally, in white society changed as well. Historically speaking, an examination of the rise of slavery in English North America reveals the hardships the victims of the Atlantic slave trade faced in trying to adapt to their new homes in the Americas. It also reveals how the slave trade became self-perpetuating as colonial America came to fulfill, with brutal efficiency, its role in the triangular trade.

Workers harvest tobacco on a Virginia plantation in the early 1600s.

Early Cheap Labor in the Colonies

When tobacco growers in Virginia and elsewhere in colonial America perceived the need for increased amounts of cheap labor, they first considered exploiting the local natives—the Indians. However, it did not take long for the whites to realize that the Native Americans were going to be very difficult to enslave. The colonists "were outnumbered," American historian Howard Zinn points out, "and while, with superior firearms, they could massacre Indians, they would face massacre in return. They could not capture them and keep them enslaved [because] the Indians were tough, resourceful, defiant, and at home in the woods, as the transplanted Englishmen were not."[12]

Moreover, superior white technology, including firearms and metal plows, did not prove effective in forcing the Indians to work on white farms. "If you were a colonist," historian Edmund Morgan writes,

> your superior technology had proved insufficient to extract anything. The Indians, keeping to themselves, laughed at your superior methods and lived from the land more abundantly and with less labor than you did. . . . So you killed the Indians, tortured them, burned their villages, burned their cornfields. It proved your superiority, in spite of your failures. . . . But you still did not grow much corn.[13]

It soon became clear that acquiring and using black African slaves would be considerably easier than enslaving the Native Americans. First, the colonists did not have to go out and capture the blacks, who came to the colonies already subdued and in chains. Also, to the black Africans the American colonies were a strange, frightening new land, a wilderness filled with potential dangers. Even if they escaped their white masters, they would be at the mercy of the natives, who knew the woods and were armed with hatchets, lances, knives, and other weapons. It was unlikely, therefore, that black slaves would risk trying to escape the colonial farms on which they worked.

Perhaps these were among the reasons that some colonists in Jamestown, in Virginia, bought twenty black slaves from a Dutch slave trader in 1619. These twenty Africans were the first blacks to arrive in colonial America. Almost every year thereafter, more

A Dutch slave ship arrives in Jamestown, carrying the first blacks to arrive in America.

African slaves arrived in the English colonies. However, at first the slave trade made little impact in the colonies because the number of slaves remained relatively low. This was partly because the English distrusted workers, and people in general, who were foreign-born and did not know English ways and language.

Also, indentured servitude, utilizing white Europeans, was still both popular and preferable in the colonies. Indentured servants voluntarily signed contracts in which they promised to work a certain number of years. In return, the servants received small amounts of money or land. In general, the concept behind indentured servitude was that the landowners temporarily owned the servants' labor, but did not own the servants themselves. Indentured servants already spoke the language. Because their service was voluntary, they were not likely to attempt escape. Finally, indentured servants could eventually be expected to assimilate into white society.

English Involvement in the Slave Trade

The many black African slaves who arrived in colonial America in the late 1600s and early 1700s were carried primarily by English slave traders. It was in this period that England became heavily involved in the trade, with ships leaving for Africa from London, Bristol, and Liverpool regularly. Between 1720 and 1730, for instance, British slave ships transported more than 100,000 slaves from West Africa to the Americas. Of these, about 40,000 went to Jamaica, about 20,000 to Barbados, and at least 10,000 to Virginia, South Carolina, and other mainland colonies. During these years, London merchants sponsored between fifty and sixty ships a year, Bristol investors between thirty and forty ships, and Liverpool traders just over ten. A single wealthy English trader, Humphrey Morice, owned a fleet of eight slave ships, which he named after his wife and daughters.

For these reasons, white indentured servants remained the labor-intensive backbone of large colonial farms between 1620 and 1660. The number of imported African blacks remained fairly low. In 1625, for example, six years after the first twenty slaves had arrived in Virginia, that colony's census listed only twenty-three resident blacks. And as late as the mid-1650s, only a few hundred blacks lived in the combined Virginia and Maryland settlements.

Fellow Sufferers Rather than Inferiors

These early blacks worked alongside indentured servants and other poor white laborers. Usually both white and black workers put in the same number of hours in an average day or average week. On many farms in Virginia and nearby colonies, black and white laborers shared the same bunkhouses, ate the same food, and on occasion had children together. The few black Africans scattered around the colonies were viewed by poor whites more as fellow sufferers than as inferiors. Overt racism based on skin color had not yet become a significant factor in the social situation of black slaves.

It is therefore not surprising that at first some black slaves gained their freedom just as white indentured servants did. In 1668 in Virginia's Northampton County, for instance, almost 30 percent of local blacks had gained their freedom. Some had borrowed money from their masters and purchased their freedom with it. Once free, the former slave got a paying job and over time paid back the debt. A few slaves petitioned the local courts to obtain their freedom. Typically they argued that, like white indentured servants, they had worked a number of years faithfully and to their masters' financial benefit; it was only fair and fitting that said term of service should entitle them to eventual freedom. Still other black slaves enjoyed freedom because they came from mixed marriages. When a white man married a black female slave, the mixed-race children were legally free.

In addition to having the legal right to borrow money, petition the courts, and gain their freedom, black slaves in early colonial times could own their own land. Evidence has survived from Northampton County showing that between 1664 and 1677, thirteen of the county's 101 black residents owned their own farms. In addition, most blacks owned livestock and some had their own black slaves.

The fact that some black slaves gained their freedom, coupled with the reality that some former slaves owned their own black slaves, reveals an important aspect of the Atlantic slave trade in early colonial America—namely, the trade was not yet a significant economic force in the colonies. There were not enough free black workers and farmers competing with white workers and farmers to make whites feel threatened

A certificate of indenture for a former slave named Shadrach appears here. His freedom was purchased by a Pennsylvania farmer in exchange for eleven years of service as an apprentice.

by blacks. As long as this situation prevailed, the transatlantic trade in Africans remained centered far to the south, in the exploitation colonies of the Caribbean and Central and South America.

A Dramatic Increase in Slave Numbers

But this situation was not destined to prevail. The late 1600s witnessed an enormous increase in the number of African slaves shipped to colonial America. One reason for this increase was a major reduction in the number of white indentured servants available from Europe. Economic prosperity was rapidly expanding in England, in part because of the success of the slave trade and English plantations on Barbados and elsewhere. As a result, more lower-class English workers were able to find jobs, either in their homeland or abroad, so they felt no need to sign themselves into servitude. Other factors reducing the number of indentured servants included a declining birthrate in England and the creation of many construction jobs following a great fire in London in 1666.

To make up for this shortfall of indentured servants in the colonies, landowners began buying more African slaves. The dramatic turnaround can be seen in surviving records from York County, in Virginia. There, the ratio of white indentured servants to black slaves fell from two servants for each slave in 1680 to fourteen slaves for each servant in 1690.

Dutch, French, Portuguese, and other slave traders were more than happy to meet the new demands for black slaves in England's American colonies. At first, the biggest concentration of new slaves was in the so-called tidewater colonies of Virginia and Maryland. Virginia's census records indicate that in 1671, the colony had about 2,000 blacks, roughly 5 percent of the overall population of 40,000. By 1700 there were 16,000 blacks in Virginia, making up more than 30 percent of the population. And by 1756 the colony had about 120,000 blacks, accounting for more than 40 percent of the overall population. Moreover, during these same years, the number of black slaves increased in every English colony south of Maryland.

In New York, Massachusetts, and other northern colonies, by contrast, no significant plantation economy developed. So there was far less need for importing African slaves. Nevertheless, some northerners did buy slaves for use in small-scale farming or manufactur-

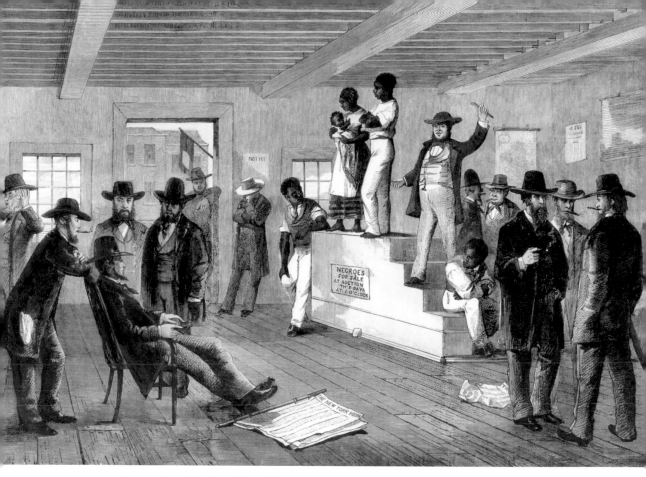

A woodcut depicts slaves being auctioned in the 1800s in Virginia.

ing. By 1746 Massachusetts had some 5,200 black slaves out of a total population of just over 224,000; and in 1749 Rhode Island had about 3,070 blacks out of its total population of about 31,500.

One important reason that so many American colonists could afford to buy large numbers of African slaves was that the price per slave decreased noticeably in the late 1600s and early 1700s. This drop in price was most attributable to a dramatic increase in England's participation and share in the Atlantic slave trade. Portugal, Spain, the Netherlands, and France had long dominated the trade. But in 1674 an English corporation, the Royal African Company, began shipping slaves directly from West Africa to colonial America, as well as to England's Caribbean colonies. The company quickly acquired what amounted to a monopoly in the slave markets of these colonies by offering special deals to fellow Englishmen. As one scholar tells it, in a market in which the Portuguese and Dutch were

charging twenty-five English pounds for a slave, the Royal African
Company

> announced that if persons could contract to receive whole
> cargoes [of black slaves] upon their arrival [in the Americas]
> and to accept all slaves between 12 and 20 years of age who

Blacks were often depicted as less than human, as can be seen in this
poster which advertises a raffle for a horse and a slave girl.

A Slave Becomes a Poet

Although all Africans who became caught up in the Atlantic slave trade were initially treated like commodities rather than people, on occasion a slave was fortunate enough to fall in with kind, socially progressive masters. This was the case with Phillis Wheatley, a slave who became renowned for her poetry. Kidnapped from her village in West Africa, she landed in Boston in July 1761, when she was eight years old. At a local slave auction, a local merchant named John Wheatley purchased her as a personal maid to his wife. The couple immediately realized that the young black woman had a voracious appetite for learning. They and their daughter tutored her in English, Latin, Greek, geography, history, and other academic subjects. With the family's aid, Phillis published her first poem in 1767 when she was just fourteen. In 1773 the Wheatleys sent Phillis to London, where she published *Poems on Various Subjects, Religious and Moral*. On returning to Boston, she received her freedom but continued to live with the Wheatley family. She later married a free black man named John Peters and died in poverty in 1784 at the age of thirty-one.

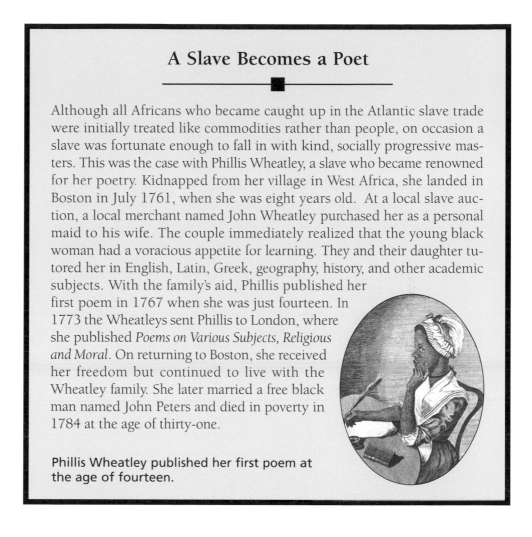

Phillis Wheatley published her first poem at the age of fourteen.

were able to go over the ship's side unaided, they would be supplied at a rate of 15 English pounds per head in Barbados, 17 pounds in Jamaica, and 18 pounds in Virginia.[14]

A Permanently Enslaved Underclass

As a result of these changes, in the first two decades of the eighteenth century more than twice as many black Africans arrived in colonial America as had been transported there in the entire previous century. Moreover, the attitudes of white colonists toward black workers had changed. No longer did lower-class white workers see blacks as fellow sufferers. The large ratios of blacks to whites, especially in the southern colonies, made blacks seem more threatening. Both white slaveholders and white workers increasingly worried not only about slave uprisings, but also about freed blacks intermarrying with whites and taking paying jobs from white workers.

White society therefore clamped down on its former reasonably lenient social and legal treatment of blacks. Blacks who arrived on slave ships could no longer look forward to the possibility of earning their freedom. More and more, whites treated the slaves as a mere commodity, which had the effect of dehumanizing blacks more thoroughly than ever before. Newspaper ads for newly arrived slaves typically depicted them as subhuman. An ad in the June 6, 1763, issue of the *Newport Gazette* read:

Legal Codes Governing Black Slaves

——————————■——————————

In the late 1600s and early 1700s various English colonies passed comprehensive legal codes covering many different aspects of the slave trade and the treatment and control of black slaves in white society. South Carolina's sweeping "black code," enacted in 1696 and titled *Act for the Better Ordering and Governing of Negroes and Slaves*, stated in part:

> Whereas, the plantations and estates of this province cannot be well and sufficiently managed and brought into use without the labor and service of Negroes and other slaves [a reference to Native Americans]; and [because] the said Negroes and other slaves brought into . . . this province for that purpose are of barbarous, wild, savage natures, and such as renders them wholly unqualified to be governed by the laws, customs, and practices of this province [we declare that] it is absolutely necessary that such [laws] and [rules] be made and enacted for the good of regulating and [controlling said slaves].

Quoted in John B. Boles, *Black Southerners, 1619–1869*. Lexington: University Press of Kentucky, 1985, p. 23.

On Thursday last arrived from the coast of Africa, the brig *Royal Charlotte* with a parcel of extremely fine, healthy, well-limbed Gold Coast slaves—men, women, boys, and girls. Gentlemen in town and country have now an opportunity to furnish themselves with such [slaves] as will suit them. [The slaves] are to be seen [and inspected] on the vessel at Taylor's wharf.[15]

One way that whites ensured that all blacks shipped in from Africa would be kept in a permanently enslaved underclass was to severely tighten local laws pertaining to blacks. For example, before the late 1600s Virginia had considered mixed-race offspring of a white father and black mother to be free. But a new law erased this loophole. All children born in this colony were now viewed as either enslaved or free based solely on the race of the mother. Furthermore, another new law stated that any "white man or woman being free who shall intermarry with a negro, mulatto, or Indian"[16] was to be banished from the colony.

Going hand-in-hand with the expansion of the slave trade and dehumanization of blacks in colonial America was a sharp increase in overt racism and utter disdain for the slaves. Racial prejudice was a way for whites to avoid having to take moral responsibility for the evils of the ongoing Atlantic slave trade. As incoming African slaves "were overpowered, mistreated, and finally murdered in the Americas," Burnside and Robotham write,

the [white] aggressors shielded themselves from the full comprehension of their brutality by rationalizing that the slaves were ignorant heathens who were somehow less [human] than [the whites] and who need not be accorded the same consideration as Christian whites. In time, the vast majority of those involved in the slave trade would choose to quiet the rumblings of conscience through such cultural and racial stereotyping, so much so that when the [U.S. Constitution] was ratified in 1789, a black slave was counted as only three-fifths of a person—two-fifths less of a human being than his white master.[17]

Thus, although the transatlantic slave trade came later to colonial America than it did to the Caribbean and South America, it eventually became deeply entrenched in the economic and social life of the region that became the United States.

Chapter Three

Acquiring Slaves in Africa

Whether they ended up in the English North American colonies or the sugar and spice plantations in the Caribbean and Central and South America, almost all the slaves carried across the Atlantic came from the same general region—West Africa. Throughout the four centuries of the slave trade, this very large region encompassed numerous separate nations, kingdoms, tribes, and peoples. Indeed, modern scholars have so far identified at least 173 African city-states, tribes, or groups that participated in or were affected by the Atlantic slave trade at one time or another.

Of these 173 groups, at least sixty-eight qualified as full-fledged nations, each with its own political history, government, and military institution that enabled it to challenge and at times dominate its neighbors. Among the most organized and powerful of these nations were the Songhai Empire and Bamana Empire, both in what is now Mali; the Jolof Empire, Denanke Kingdom, and Kingdom of Saalum, in present-day Senegal; the Kingdom of Dahomey in what is now Benin; the Kuba Kingdom and Luba Empire, in today's Democratic Republic of Congo; and the Kingdom of Ndongo, in what is now Angola.

The diverse nations and tribes of West Africa belonged to about forty-five distinct ethnic groups. Chief among them were the Yoruba, Wolof, Igbo, Akan, Chamba, Makua, BaKongo, Gbe, and Mbundu. Each spoke a different language, usually a dialect of the primary mother-tongue of central and western Africa—Niger-Congo, of which Bantu is a major branch. The fact that each ethnic group had a different language and quite often different customs worked against those who were sold into slavery. Whenever possible, white slave traders and masters tried to mix members of two, three, or more ethnic groups together. That made it hard for the slaves to communicate; disoriented them, thereby rendering them easier to manage; and made it logistically difficult for the slaves on a given ship or plantation to band together and coordinate large-scale rebellions or escapes.

African vs. European Slavery

One thing that most of the nations and ethnic groups of West Africa had in common was that in one way or another they played an active role in the Atlantic slave trade. Africans regularly captured and sold other Africans, either to neighboring nations or to white slave traders. The fact was that slavery was an age-old institution that had existed in West Africa long before white slave traders arrived.

The chief route into slavery in Africa, both before and after the arrival of the whites, was to be captured in war. Once the European demand for blacks slaves was established, it was not unusual for one African group to make war on another primarily to obtain captives that could be sold to the whites. In other cases, members of one African group kidnapped residents of neighboring nations or villages. Such raids sometimes provoked wars of revenge, which produced still more slaves for one side or the other. Usually, the aggressors marched the captives overland to the coast, where the Europeans had constructed beachheads and forts.

It is important to emphasize that, although the peoples of West Africa practiced slavery, there were significant differences between the African and European versions of the institution. African slaves were similar in many ways to European indentured servants. They received small wages for their labors and had the option of eventually gaining their freedom. According to John Newton (born 1725), a British slave trader who later became an abolitionist,

Captured Africans are led to the coast to be sold as slaves. Africans frequently sold other Africans into slavery.

The state of slavery among these wild, barbarous people, as we esteem them, is much milder than in our colonies. For as, on the one hand, they have no land in high cultivation, like [in] our West Indies [Caribbean] plantations, and therefore no call for that excessive, [unceasing] labor which exhausts our slaves. So, on the other hand, no [African master] is permitted to draw blood even from a slave.[18]

Also, African slaves worked as artisans as well as menial laborers and quite often became trusted members of their masters' families and respected members of their communities.

A Healthy Respect for the Natives

The transition from African slavery to European slavery, which was far more harsh and inhumane, was therefore a great shock to those Africans who were taken to the coast and sold to white traders. But neither the Europeans nor the black African slave runners they dealt with cared that the slaves were about to enter a more brutal system. Certainly all the white traders cared about was acquiring as many slaves as they could for the cheapest prices possible.

During the negotiations, the European agents as a rule held their African counterparts in contempt. The general white view was that the blacks, no matter how wealthy and powerful they might be in their own nations, were savages who were inferior to whites in every way. An English slave trader known to history only as Owen stated in his journal: "These people that go by the names of kings and princes are only so in title. Their substance consists of nothing more than a lace hat, a gown, and silver-headed cane . . . to distinguish them from the rest of the Negroes."[19]

A Muslim Caught Up in the Slave Trade

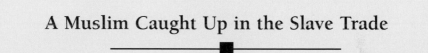

In the 1700s at the height of the slave trade, so many people were haphazardly captured and sold into slavery that on occasion some of the slave traders themselves ended up in bondage. This was what happened to Ayuba Suleiman Diallo, also known as Job ben Solomon. Born in about 1700 in the land of Bondu, in what is now Mali, in West Africa, Diallo was a well-educated Muslim merchant who sometimes dealt in black slaves. In 1730 he sold some slaves to a British trader near the coast. On his way home, Diallo and his two assistants were captured by African tribesmen, who sold the three Muslims to the very same Englishman Diallo had recently dealt with. Diallo ended up on a tobacco plantation in Maryland, where he spent two years before a white merchant recognized that he was an educated Muslim. The merchant took him to Britain, where some wealthy men who were impressed with Diallo bought his freedom. He then returned to Africa, where he was reunited with his family.

Nevertheless, this contempt for the natives had to be tempered with a healthy respect for their military prowess and ability to defend themselves. Modern depictions of European slavers heading inland, attacking native villages, and dragging hundreds of captives to the coast are largely fictional. Such raids did occur occasionally in certain areas where and when the situation allowed. But for the most part, the local black societies were in full control of their territories, including the coastal regions. "Aware that the [white] seafarers meant to exploit their wealth," Burnside and Robotham point out,

> the Africans hastened to secure their coasts and inland waterways. Skilled warriors, expert fishermen, and seasoned navigators of the uncharted waters, the West Africans were virtually invincible—and they could prove it if necessary. They owned large canoes capable of carrying twenty or thirty men, more than the total crew of many European ships

Depictions of white slavers attacking African villages and dragging off captives to be sold as slaves are largely fictional.

that reached their shores. Indeed, those Europeans who survived the arduous sea voyage [to West Africa] did not have the resources to meet such a contest. Arriving in small vessels battered by the high seas, with scant crews and few guns, they might hope to intimidate the locals but were clearly no match for a contingent of African warriors.[20]

Another powerful deterrent to white slavers venturing inland was fear of catching exotic diseases, including malaria.

The March to the Coast

Thus, the first time that most African slaves saw a white person was when they arrived on the Atlantic coast after a forced march from an inland region. The vast majority of these unfortunate individuals remain faceless, nameless, and silent to history. However, one of their number did manage to survive capture, enslavement, and the voyage across the ocean and to record his experiences in writing. His name was Olaudah Equiano. He was captured in what is now southern Nigeria in the 1750s:

> One day, when all our people were gone out to their work as usual and only I and my dear sister were left to mind the house, two men and a woman got over our walls and in a moment seized us both, and without giving us time to cry out or make resistance, they stopped [gagged] our mouths and ran off with us into the nearest wood. Here, they tied our hands and continued to carry us as far as they could till night came on, when we reached a small house where the robbers halted. . . . We were then unbound but were unable to take any food, and being quite overpowered by fatigue and grief, our only relief was some sleep.[21]

During their march overland toward the coast, slaves like Equiano were almost always shackled to discourage escape. A Scottish doctor and explorer named Mungo Park, who visited the western African coast in the 1790s, described the standard manner of shackling:

> They [the slaves] are commonly secured by putting the right leg of one and the left of another into the same pair of fetters. By supporting the fetters with a string, they can walk,

A long line of slaves marches toward a new and terrible future.

though very slowly. Every four slaves are likewise fastened together by the necks with a strong rope of twisted thongs, and in the night an additional pair of fetters is put on their hands, and sometimes a light iron chain passed round their necks. [22]

The slaves' misery caused by these brutal and uncomfortable methods was compounded by their fear, once they realized they would be sold to white people, that they would be eaten by the Europeans. Park later described a conversation he had with a group of prisoners:

They were all very inquisitive, but they viewed me at first with looks of horror and repeatedly asked if my countrymen were cannibals. They were very desirous to know what became of the slaves after they had crossed the salt water. I told them they were employed in cultivating the land, but they would not believe me. One of them, putting his hand upon the ground, said with great simplicity, "Have you really got such ground as this to set your feet upon?" A deeply rooted idea, that the whites purchase Negroes for the purpose of devouring them . . . naturally makes the slaves contemplate a journey towards the coast with great terror. [23]

Whatever fears and expectations the slaves harbored during the forced march, they quickly learned that any resistance, or even inadvertent mistakes, would be met with severe punishment. Park's account contains a description of the harsh treatment of a clumsy slave:

One of the Serawoolli slaves dropped a load from his head, for which he was smartly whipped. The load was replaced, but he had not proceeded above a mile before he let it fall a second time, for which he received the same punishment. After this, he traveled in great pain until about two o'clock, when we stopped. . . . The poor slave was now so completely exhausted that he lay motionless on the ground. [24]

Park went on to explain that the wounded slave soon died and his body was left to rot in the jungle.

Sold to White Traders

Once the slaves arrived at the coast, they were sold to white slave merchants. In exchange for the slaves, the whites paid the local slave runners such items as barrels of brandy, wine, and rum; tobacco plants; gunpowder; hats and other clothing items; pewter plates, bowls, and spoons; and swords and knives.

The whites learned early in the game that the native negotiators were far from gullible and very difficult to cheat. Captain Jean Barbot, a Frenchman who worked on English slave ships, later remembered, with some degree of disdain, the savvy displayed by native traders:

You discover daily that the natives have a splendid mental capacity with much judgment and sharp and ready apprehension, which immediately understands whatever you suggest. They have so good a memory that it is beyond comprehension, and although they cannot read or write, they are admirably well organized in their trading and never get mixed up. I have seen one of the brokers on board trading four ounces of gold with fifteen different persons and making each a different bargain, without making any mistakes or appearing the least harassed.[25]

After the sale was complete, the slaves were usually held in pens until they could be inspected and loaded onto slave ships. In some cases, these pens were inside forts built by white traders on

African slaves are shackled and loaded into the cargo hold of a slave ship.

A Slave Writes an Account of His Capture

Few eyewitness accounts of the slave trade by the black slaves themselves have survived. One of the most substantial and famous of these accounts is that by Olaudah Equiano, also known as Gustavus Vasa. Born in 1745 in what is now Nigeria, at about the age of ten he was kidnapped by black African tribesmen and taken to the Atlantic coast. Equiano managed to survive the brutal middle passage across the ocean and ended up in Barbados. Not long afterward, he was sold to a planter in Virginia. After only three months, a British naval officer purchased him and took him along on various military expeditions. During this period, Equiano learned English and became a first-rate seaman. In 1762 he was sold to a Quaker who allowed him to earn his freedom. Once free, Equiano made England his home and became involved in the abolitionist movement. At the urging of abolitionist friends, he wrote *The Interesting Narrative of Olaudah Equiano,* which described his capture and harrowing experiences in slavery. The book was published in 1789 and became a best seller. Equiano died in 1797 at the age of fifty-two.

After gaining his freedom, Olaudah Equiano wrote an account of his life as a slave.

or near the beaches. These strongholds were intended to house the ship captains and their officers comfortably and make their trading activities easier. The forts were equipped with cannons and other weaponry. These guns were usually set up not on the landward side, since raids by the local natives with whom the masters of the forts were trading were extremely rare, but facing the sea. In that position the cannons created a deterrent against rival white traders who might suddenly sail into view and try to

A Slave's Journey to the Seacoast

———————————◼———————————

In a book published in 1789, former slave Olaudah Equiano described his months-long journey across West Africa after he and his sister were captured in their village. Eventually, as told in this excerpt, they reached the Atlantic coast.

> All the nations and people I had hitherto [before this] passed through resembled our own in their manner, customs, and language, but I came at length to a country the inhabitants of which differed from us in all those particulars. [They] ate without washing their hands. They cooked also in iron pots and had European cutlasses and crossbows, which were unknown to us. . . . At last I came to the banks of a large river, which was covered with canoes in which the people appeared to live with their household utensils. . . . I was put into one of these canoes and we began to paddle and move along the river. . . . Thus I continued to travel, sometimes by land, sometimes by water, through different countries and various nations, till at the end of six or seven months after I had been kidnapped I arrived at the seacoast.

Quoted in Paul Edwards, ed., *Equiano's Travels*. Oxford: Harcourt, 1996, pp. 13–14.

steal valuable slaves. Jean Barbot left behind this vivid description of the English fort at Cabo Corso ("Cape Coast") on the so-called Gold Coast, now in the country of Ghana:

> Its shape is quadrangular. It is built of locally baked brick and black stone, and is situated on a point which juts out so that it is only connected to the mainland on its northern side. The rocks in the sea surrounding it make it almost inaccessible, because the sea breaks furiously on them. . . . There is a little bay formed by the rocks on the east side, where longboats enter and are beached on the sand. This, however, does not pose any threat to the castle, which commands this landing place with 16 large 18-pounder iron cannon and with the small arms of the garrison [guards].

[Also] the walls are tall and thick. The lodgings inside the castle are very comfortable and spacious. . . . The most notable item is the slave house, which lies below ground. It consists of vaulted cellars, divided into several apartments which can easily hold a thousand slaves. [26]

The next step was to load the slaves onto ships for the next leg in the triangular trade, the voyage across the ocean, known as the middle passage. Decade after decade, century after century, English, Portuguese, French, Dutch, and other European traders maintained their African beachheads and forts and loaded their ships with human cargo. This insidious enterprise would have been impossible without the aid and participation of local African rulers, who at the time did not grasp the large-scale harm they were doing. "The Europeans exploited Africa's human resources to the extent that they could within the boundaries set by Africa's rulers," Burnside and Robotham write. "This pattern of material interaction and cross-cultural exchange would continue into the nineteenth century, to be broken only when Africa's true wealth—her population—was profoundly depleted." [27]

Chapter Four

The Dreaded Middle Passage

Once the slaves from Africa's interior reached the coast and were sold to a white slave trader, their fate was grim. They had to suffer the indignity of a physical inspection similar to that given to livestock. Then they were packed into the hold of a vessel waiting to transport them across the ocean, where they would be forced to do the bidding of new owners. Never again would they see their family and friends or set foot in their native lands.

Though this fate was sad and cruel in itself, even more appalling were the realities of the journey across the Atlantic—the dreaded middle passage. The conditions onboard the slave ships were horrifying. William Wilberforce (born 1759), one of Britain's leading abolitionists, summed them up this way: "Never can so much misery be found condensed in so small a place as in a slave ship during the middle passage."[28]

A substantial portion of those who were forced to undertake these terrifying voyages died in the crossing. Overcrowding, physical abuse, disease, storms, suicides, rebellions, and other misfortunes all took an awful toll. For this reason, the middle passage was risky not only for the slaves but also for the slave traders, who lost money on each captive who did not complete the trip to the Americas.

Loading the Slave Ships

To ensure that as many slaves as possible completed the voyage intact, the white slave traders carefully inspected each captive who arrived on the coast. Those that seemed sickly or weak and therefore unlikely to survive the middle passage were rejected. A Dutch trader named Willem Bosman, who in the late 1600s witnessed

The brutal practice of branding slaves is carried out before leaving the African continent.

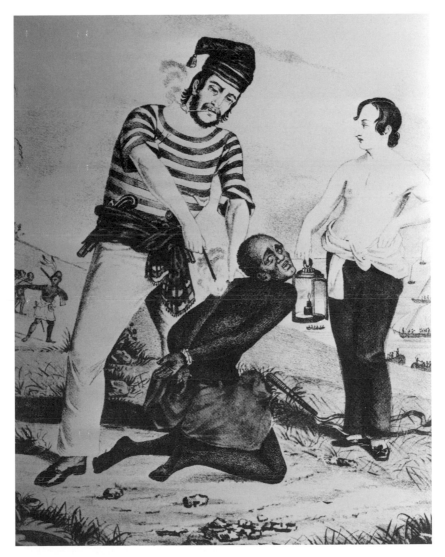

the inspection and loading of slaves onto ships for the middle passage, wrote:

> [The captives] are all brought out together in a large plain, where they are thoroughly examined by our surgeons, even to the smallest member, both men and women naked, without the least distinction or modesty. Those approved as good are set on one side, and the lame and faulty are set by as invalids, which are here called macrons.

The slaves who passed the inspection were then branded with hot irons, Bosman recalled: "This is done that we may distinguish them from the slaves of the English, French, or others." Though such practice might "seem very barbarous," he added, it was "necessary." [29]

While the white guards and sailors loaded the inspected and branded slaves onto the ship, they also loaded the large food stores that would be needed during the long voyage. Whenever possible, the ship captains obtained a food staple that the captives were accustomed to eating. That way there was less chance that the slaves would get sick and die during the voyage, thereby creating a financial loss for the owners. In many parts of West Africa, the leading staple was yams. So slave traders negotiated deals to buy large supplies of yams from local chieftains. The sellers ran hard bargains for the yams, just as they did for the slaves themselves, in this case demanding fixed numbers of copper and iron bars as payment. The French captain Jean Barbot estimated that a store of some 100,000 yams was necessary to sustain a shipload of 500 slaves during the Atlantic crossing. The slave traders also bought wood, fresh water, and goats and hogs (to supply milk and meat for the ship's crew) from the local natives.

Nightmarish Conditions Below Decks

With the slaves and provisions loaded, a slave ship embarked on the middle passage. Very few eyewitness accounts of this terrible journey written by Africans who actually suffered through the ordeal have survived. This is not surprising, since most of them either died on the voyage or went on to live the rest of their lives as illiterate slaves in the Americas.

Among the handful of slaves who gained their freedom, got an education, and later wrote about the experience was Olaudah

Slaves taken from a captured trading ship show clear signs of starvation and mistreatment.

Equiano, who had been kidnapped from his village and marched to the coast. His description of the middle passage is both riveting and revealing. Particularly memorable, he said, was the stench in the ship's hold, where hundreds of prisoners lay or sat shackled, sweating, vomiting, and in some cases bleeding from various skin sores. "I was soon put down under the decks," Equiano wrote, "and there I received such a salutation in my nostrils as I had never experienced in my life. So that with the loathsomeness of the stench and [people] crying together, I became so sick and low that I was not able to eat." Instead of understanding why Equiano had no appetite, his guards cruelly punished him for his refusal to eat. "One of them held me fast by the hands," he said, "and laid me across I think the windlass, and tied my feet while the other flogged me severely. I had never experienced anything of this kind before." [30]

The packed, smelly conditions below decks were also described by Alexander Falconbridge, a British ship doctor, in 1788. "The height, sometimes, between decks," he wrote,

> was only 18 inches [46cm], so that the unfortunate human beings could not turn around, or even on their sides, the elevation being less than the breadth of their shoulders. And here they are usually chained to the decks by the neck and legs. In such a place, the sense of misery and suffocation is so great that the Negroes . . . are driven to frenzy.[31]

During the voyage, small groups of slaves would be allowed to spend some time on deck in the open air. These moments of comfort were brief, however; soon the prisoners were forced to return to the nightmarish conditions below, as Equiano recalled:

> The closeness of the place and the heat of the climate, added to the number [of prisoners] in the ship, which was so crowded that each had scarcely room to turn himself, almost suffocated us. This produced copious [plentiful] perspiration, so that the air soon became unfit for respiration from a variety of loathsome smells and brought on a sickness among the slaves, of which many died.

These unfortunate individuals were callously tossed overboard. Many of the other slaves came to long for death, including Equiano himself, who "began to hope" that death "would soon put an end to my miseries."[32]

Suicides and Rebellions

In fact, a few of the slaves who shared the ship with Equiano went so far as to attempt suicide. He wrote: "One day, when we had a smooth sea and moderate wind, two of my wearied countrymen who were chained together" managed to rush past the guards and "jumped into the sea." Seeing this, another prisoner who was then on deck also hurled himself overboard. "I believe many more [of the prisoners] would very soon have done the same," Equiano wrote, "if they had not been prevented by the ship's crew, who were instantly alarmed." Two of the three who had jumped overboard drowned, while the third was rescued and then savagely beaten "for thus attempting to prefer death to slavery."[33]

A Description of a Slave Ship

———■———

European slave traders who wrote accounts of the middle passage often painted the conditions endured by the slaves aboard the ships in rosier terms than the much darker and crueler reality. Typical was this excerpt from a report by an English doctor, George Pinckard, who inspected several slave ships.

Divided into two crowded parties, they [the slaves] reposed during the night upon the bare planks below—the males on the main deck, the females upon the deck of the aft cabin. In the daytime they were not allowed to remain in the place where they had slept, but were kept mostly upon the open deck, where they were made to exercise. . . . We saw them dance and heard them sing. In dancing, they scarcely moved their feet, and threw about their arms and twisted and writhed their bodies into a multitude of disgusting and indecent attitudes. . . . [They] seemed happy. . . . I am most happy to conclude my report of this visit by informing you that we discovered no marks of those horrors and cruelties said to be practiced on board the ships.

Quoted in Thomas Howard, ed., *Black Voyage: Eyewitness Accounts of the Atlantic Slave Trade.* Boston: Little, Brown, 1971, pp. 106–7.

Many of the slaves were so traumatized and/or exhausted by their ordeal that they lacked the energy and gumption to kill themselves or to resist their captors in any meaningful way. However, surviving evidence shows that some of them did resist, often vigorously. Violent outbursts occurred on several of the slave ships. Sometimes these escalated into full-scale rebellions, a few of which were successful or almost so. Willem Bosman described one nearly successful insurrection aboard a Dutch slave ship in the late 1600s:

Unknown to any of the ship's crew, [the male slaves] possessed themselves of a hammer, with which in a short time they broke all their fetters [and] came above deck and fell upon our men, some of whom they grievously wounded. [The slaves] would certainly have mastered [taken over] the ship if a French and English ship had not very fortunately happened to lie by us, [and hearing] our distress gun, [they] came to our assistance. About twenty of the slaves were killed. [34]

An illustration depicts a slave rebellion onboard an eighteenth-century slave ship.

In 1740 in an uprising on another Dutch ship, the *Middleburgs Welvaren,* the slaves gained control of the lower decks. The well-armed white sailors on the upper deck fired their guns downward in volley after volley, killing 213 of the 260 slaves on board, and the rebellion collapsed. A rebellion that happened ten years earlier, on an American ship, the *Little George,* was more successful. The slaves managed to get off the vessel and swim to the African coast. There they received aid from local natives and escaped recapture.

To avoid such incidents, prudent ship captains took a number of precautions, including frequent double-checking that leg irons and other restraints were secure. An English captain, Thomas Phillips, listed other steps he and his crew took to prevent insurrections:

> We always keep [guards] upon the hatchways, and have a chest of small arms, ready, loaded, and primed, constantly lying at hand on the quarter-deck, together with some [grenades] and two of our quarter deck guns pointing on the deck [toward the hold], the door of which is always kept shut and well-barred. [35]

After an unsuccessful rebellion, the captain and his guards meted out severe punishments to the ringleaders. Flogging with whips or ropes was common, as was applying thumbscrews (a device that twisted metal screws into a person's thumbnails). Some rebellious slave leaders were shot, thrown overboard, or dismembered (cut into pieces). In 1788 aboard a British ship, the *Ruby,* a rebellious slave was first stabbed and clubbed until he was unconscious. Then the captain, who was widely known for his sadism, ordered the man chained to the mast without food or water. The bound slave's skin peeled off in the hot sun, and at the end of the third day he died.

An Incredible Death Toll

Suicides and rebellions were not the only factors that contributed to the horrible death toll of the average Atlantic middle passage. The average death rate, which modern scholars estimate at 12 to 22 percent of the slaves aboard each ship, was also partly caused by extreme overcrowding. On some ships the slaves were packed so tightly in the hold that some of them lay directly on top of others. Such unfortunate individuals died when they simply could not breathe any longer or, unable to keep food down in the stinking, unsanitary conditions, starved to death.

Disease was another major factor in the onboard death toll during the transatlantic slave voyages. According to Johannes Postma:

> Germs could be carried aboard undetected and slaves weakened from malnutrition and other hardships were more susceptible to disease. Larger slave ships usually had a doctor and surgeons on board, but they could do very little to prevent or cure disease. As the eighteenth century progressed, traders learned that consumption of citrus fruit could prevent scurvy [a disease caused by lack of vitamin C], and ship doctors also began to inoculate against smallpox. These measures contributed to the decline of mortality rates on slave ships. [36]

In addition to scurvy and smallpox, many slaves, along with some white crew members, contracted yellow fever. In fact, it was slave ships that transferred yellow fever from Africa to the Americas in the first place. Typically, the mosquitoes that carry the disease bred in standing water in onboard cisterns and barrels. Both slaves and crew also frequently came down with ophthalmia, an eye disease that can cause temporary blindness. Some ships veered off course or even ran aground because the entire crew had been stricken with ophthalmia.

Lack of water was still another cause of death during the middle passage. With hundreds of slaves and crew members on a slave ship, the need for fresh water was acute; however, most slave ships lacked the room to carry proper supplies of water. On average, each slave required eight to ten pints of fresh water daily, but on most slave ships the allotment per slave was only two pints per day. James Arnold, a surgeon who served aboard the *Ruby,* estimated that the captives on that vessel were given a mere one pint of water each day. The result, not surprisingly, was severe dehydration, which caused great discomfort, psychological depression, and in some cases death.

In addition to suicide, overcrowding, disease, and insufficient water, another factor in the high death toll during the Atlantic crossings was a general disregard for the lives of the slaves, who were typically viewed as subhuman and therefore disposable. A famous case of such prejudice, enhanced by blatant cruelty, occurred on the *Zong*, a British slave ship that made the Atlantic crossing in 1781. After many days at sea, the vessel was short of water and many of the slaves onboard were sick with various diseases. The captain, Luke Collingwood, made the decision to toss 133 of the weakest, sickest slaves into the ocean and let them drown. He later claimed that this was the only way to ensure that the crew and remaining slaves would have enough water for the rest of the voyage. The incident enraged abolitionists, whose cause was gaining strength at the time.

It must be noted that the black slaves were not the only ones who suffered and contributed to the overall death tolls on these dangerous transatlantic voyages. Strict discipline among the crew was seen as essential to keeping the human cargo in line and ensuring a profitable voyage. So white sailors who broke rules, or

Hundreds of Slaves Die in a Storm

In addition to cruel treatment onboard the slave ships, the middle passage subjected the slaves to the dangers of ocean storms, which sometimes damaged or even wrecked the ships, sending many on board to watery graves. The worst such disaster on record occurred on January 1, 1738. A Dutch slave ship, the *Leusden,* was carrying 716 slaves across the Atlantic when it encountered a fierce storm that deposited the boat on some large rocks. The ship tilted and began taking on water. The white crewmen jumped into the lifeboats and most of them survived, but they left the black slaves confined in the hold. Only fourteen of the slaves survived. The disaster was such a huge financial loss that the Dutch West India Company, which had sponsored the voyage, thereafter discontinued shipping slaves across the Atlantic.

even complained too much, were usually dealt with harshly. Dr. Falconbridge recalled an incident he witnessed on one of the several trips he took on slaving ships:

> Most of the sailors were treated with brutal severity. But one in particular, a man advanced in years, experienced it in an uncommon degree. Having made some complaint relative to his allowance of water . . . one of the officers seized him and with the blows he bestowed on him beat out several of his teeth. Not content with this, while the poor old man was yet bleeding, one of the iron pump-bolts was fixed in his mouth and kept there by a piece of rope tied round his head. Being unable to spit out the blood . . . the man was almost choked. [37]

As many as 20 percent or more of the crewmen on the slave ships died of disease, brutality, or other causes, a death rate not

Slave traders toss ill and rebellious slaves overboard.

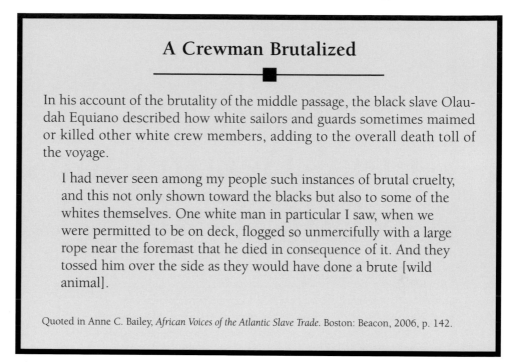

A Crewman Brutalized

In his account of the brutality of the middle passage, the black slave Olaudah Equiano described how white sailors and guards sometimes maimed or killed other white crew members, adding to the overall death toll of the voyage.

I had never seen among my people such instances of brutal cruelty, and this not only shown toward the blacks but also to some of the whites themselves. One white man in particular I saw, when we were permitted to be on deck, flogged so unmercifully with a large rope near the foremast that he died in consequence of it. And they tossed him over the side as they would have done a brute [wild animal].

Quoted in Anne C. Bailey, *African Voices of the Atlantic Slave Trade.* Boston: Beacon, 2006, p. 142.

much lower than the one suffered by the slaves. Clearly, the middle passage aboard a slave ship was a horrendous experience for both the slaves and any white crew member who ran afoul of the captain and his henchmen. The total number of slaves and crew members who never made it to the Americas during the four centuries of the slave trade is unknown. But even the most modest of modern estimates places it in the millions.

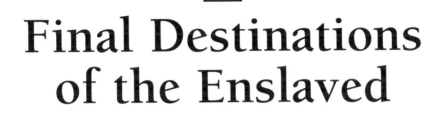

Chapter Five

Final Destinations of the Enslaved

The cruel and dehumanizing middle passage ended when a slave ship docked at a port somewhere in the Americas. In most cases the port was located near the plantations or farms on which the slaves would live and work. So the final leg of their journey was generally by foot, as they trekked overland to their new homes. In the early years of the United States, some slaves landed in Georgia or South Carolina and had to take long overland journeys to cotton plantations hundreds of miles inland.

However, as many as 10 percent of the slaves had to endure a second ocean voyage. For example, both Jamaica and Curaçao were frequently used as transitional depots for slaves bound ultimately for plantations in Colombia, Mexico, Venezuela, and Panama. Other slaves landed in Caribbean ports and within a few days or weeks were shipped northward to the English North American colonies.

The vast majority of slaves involved in the Atlantic trade landed initially in one of about sixteen primary locations. Almost all the slaves transported by English ships docked in five of the sixteen—the North American colonies extending from Georgia to Massachusetts; the English Leeward Islands; the English Windward Islands and Trinidad; Jamaica; and Barbados. Most French slave traders brought their human cargoes to St. Domingue or the French Windward Islands. The leading and most populous destination for the slaves, however, was Brazil, where more than 40 percent of the captives who suffered through the middle passage ended up. In fact, the Portuguese and some other Europeans shipped slaves from Africa to Brazil on a constant basis during the entire four centuries that the trade existed. (Even after the slave trade was abolished in the early 1800s, slavery remained legal in Brazil and was not outlawed there until 1888.)

Whatever the slaves' final destination might be, they were forced to deal with certain grim realities that became more or less standard for most African slaves. First, the slaves had to endure the humiliating experience of being sold, either at auction or via a private sale. Then they had to learn to live in a society very different from any that then existed in Africa. The slaves had to learn to follow strict rules and to expect severe punishments when they broke these rules.

A Legendary Incident

Getting the newly arrived slaves to follow the rules set down by local owners was usually fairly easy. After their long, painful voyage across the ocean, most slaves were exhausted, fearful, and therefore fairly quiet and easy to handle when they landed in the Americas. So they largely did as they were told, passively allowing their handlers to clean them up for sale and lead them off the ship and into local holding pens.

There were occasional exceptions, however. One that has become legendary occurred in 1803 on one of the islands off the coast of Georgia. A slave ship carrying a cargo of Igbos, a people native to present-day Nigeria, docked after its trip across the Atlantic. The white guards began to lead the prisoners down the gangplanks and onto the beach. The expectation was that the slaves would obediently do what they were told and that their handlers would have little trouble preparing them for the upcoming auction in which they would be sold to local planters.

What the whites did not know was that the members of this particular tribe of Igbos had a long, proud tradition of refusing to live in servitude. White onlookers were surprised, therefore, when the first few slaves who stepped onto the beach did not follow the

This large wooden pen was used as a warehouse to hold slaves before they were sold at auction.

guards. Instead, the Igbos walked, silently and purposefully, down the beach toward the open ocean. Ignoring the shouts, warnings, and whips of the guards, every man, woman, and child who left the ship followed those first few leaders in an orderly, almost robotic manner, down the beach and into the sea. The line of Igbos trod deeper and deeper into the water until every last person disappeared from view. Despite the efforts of the guards to rescue some of the slaves, all of them drowned. According to Burnside and Robotham:

> The Igbos believed their spirits [souls], guided by their ancestors, would travel home when they died, as long as their heads were not separated from their bodies. So great was their belief and their longing to return to Africa that they walked with one will into the ocean as horrified slave merchants and planters watched their profits wash away to sea. [This episode] embodies not just the tragedy of the transat-

lantic slave trade, [but also] the epic courage of a people determined to wrest [grasp] control of their destiny however they could. [38]

Like Sheep in a Fold

The incident with the Igbos and their display of undaunted courage in the face of permanent servitude was highly unusual. The vast majority of black Africans who arrived in the Americas were initially quite relieved that they had made it across the ocean alive, and they wanted to stay alive as long as they could. Many of them probably conjectured that, given time and fortunate circumstances, they might find a way to regain their freedom. In the meantime, they faced the reality of new, strange surroundings. The society of their white masters was very different from their own,

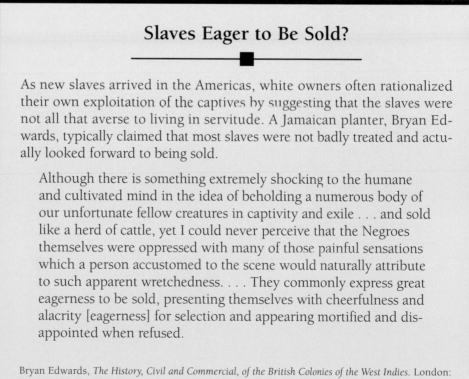

Slaves Eager to Be Sold?

As new slaves arrived in the Americas, white owners often rationalized their own exploitation of the captives by suggesting that the slaves were not all that averse to living in servitude. A Jamaican planter, Bryan Edwards, typically claimed that most slaves were not badly treated and actually looked forward to being sold.

> Although there is something extremely shocking to the humane and cultivated mind in the idea of beholding a numerous body of our unfortunate fellow creatures in captivity and exile . . . and sold like a herd of cattle, yet I could never perceive that the Negroes themselves were oppressed with many of those painful sensations which a person accustomed to the scene would naturally attribute to such apparent wretchedness. . . . They commonly express great eagerness to be sold, presenting themselves with cheerfulness and alacrity [eagerness] for selection and appearing mortified and disappointed when refused.

Bryan Edwards, *The History, Civil and Commercial, of the British Colonies of the West Indies.* London: John Stockdale, 1794, p. 42.

and they needed to learn what they could about the white world to ensure their continued survival.

This was the attitude that Olaudah Equiano adopted upon his arrival in Barbados, in the Lesser Antilles island chain, in 1757. He was immediately struck by how different the houses looked as compared to those in his native land. He was also amazed at the sight of horses, for though horses then existed in Africa, he personally had never seen one. "We were conducted immediately to the merchants' yard," he later recalled,

> where we were all pent up together like so many sheep in a fold, without regard to sex or age. As every object was new to me, everything I saw filled me with surprise. . . . But I was still more astonished on seeing people on horseback. I did not know what this could mean, and indeed I thought these people were full of nothing but magical arts. [39]

Most newly arrived slaves did not have long to sit around and muse about their strange surroundings. A majority, especially those in reasonably good physical condition, were sold as quickly as possible to planters and other white owners. One of the most common methods of sale, especially in the early years of the slave trade, was the so-called scramble. "In this practice," Johannes Postma explains, "a price and time were designated beforehand, and at the signal of the owner, the buyers rushed the slaves and claimed their choices at the standard price. The bewildered victims must have been horrified." [40] A rare eyewitness description of such a scramble sale has survived in Equiano's narrative:

> On a signal given (as the beat of a drum), the buyers rush at once into the yard where the slaves are confined and make choice of that parcel they like best. The noise and clamor with which this is attended and the eagerness visible in the [faces] of the buyers serve not a little to increase the apprehensions of the terrified Africans. In this manner, without scruple, are relations and friends separated, most of them never to see each other again. [41]

Perhaps because it was so rushed and manic, over time the scramble method became less common and was replaced by the more orderly slave auction. A contemporary description of such

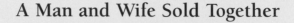

A Man and Wife Sold Together

Often, black families and married couples were separated and sold to different owners at the slave auctions that took place at the end of the middle passage. English doctor George Pinckard witnessed one heartrending exception and later described it.

In the course of the sale, a tall and robust Negro, on being brought into the auction room, approached the table with a fine Negress hanging upon his arm. The man was ordered to mount the chair. . . . The woman remained in the crowd. A certain price was mentioned to set the purchase forward and the bidding commenced. But the slave . . . sunk his chin upon his breast and hung his head in positive refusal. Then, looking at the woman, he made signs expressive of great distress. [Over time] he grew more and more restless, and repeated signs which seemed to say—"Let us be sold together." [Soon] humanity could no longer resist the appeal [and] a second chair was brought and the woman was placed at the side of her husband. . . . The bidding was renewed [and] the two were sold together for 1650 guilders.

Quoted in Thomas Howard, ed., *Black Voyage: Eyewitness Accounts of the Atlantic Slave Trade.* Boston: Little, Brown, 1971, pp. 113–14.

an auction has survived. It was written by George Pinckard, an English doctor who traveled on a number of slave ships. "A long table was placed in the middle of a large room," he recalled:

At one end was seated the auctioneer, at the other was placed a chair for the Negroes to stand upon, in order to be exposed to the view of the purchasers. . . . All being in readiness, the slaves were brought in, one at a time, and placed upon the chair before the bidders, who handled and inspected them, with as little concern as if they had been examining cattle in Smithfield Market. They turned them about, felt them, viewed their shapes and limbs, and looked into their mouths, made them jump and throw out their arms, and subjected them to all the means of trial as if dealing for a horse or other brute animal. [42]

Slaves with Multiple Masters

Whether slaves were sold in a scramble sale or an auction, their ultimate fate was the same. They had now acquired a new master, in most cases the one who would own them ever after. However, an undetermined minority of slaves who crossed the Atlantic to the Americas endured two, three, or more sales. Passed from one owner to another, they sometimes ended up crossing the ocean again, as it was not uncommon for American owners to sell off a few of their slaves to European buyers.

Here again, Equiano's experiences are instructive. Unlike most slaves who landed in the Americas, he was sold several times and traveled to lands that he had never before dreamed existed. In the Barbados scramble described in his narrative, a planter from Virginia purchased him and transported him to a plantation in that faraway colony. Equiano had barely begun to work on the plantation when an Englishman arrived. "One day," the young African later wrote,

> the captain of the merchant ship called the Industrious Bee came on some business to my master's house. This gentleman, whose name was Michael Henry Pascal . . . liked me so well that he made a purchase of me. I think I have often heard him say he gave thirty or forty pound sterling for me. . . . I was carried aboard a fine large ship, loaded with tobacco, etc., and just ready to sail for England. [43]

Pascal and two other masters who subsequently owned Equiano treated him with kindness and educated him. And he was eventually able to buy his freedom. In contrast, the vast majority of slaves did not have kind masters, never received an education, and never had the slightest chance of gaining their freedom. Instead, they became part of a large-scale, insidious system in which a few white masters controlled practically every aspect of the lives of large numbers of slaves.

Cruel Methods of Control

Indeed, as had been the case during the middle passage, control was the key to making the slave trade and slavery in general work in the Americas. Sometimes instilling a morbid fear of punishment was enough to maintain that control. It was common, for instance, for a ship captain or plantation owner to single out one slave and savagely beat him or her in front of the others. This practice was intended to set an example and thereby discourage any misbehavior by the slaves, either during their journey or after they were settled in their new homes.

However, resistance by at least some slaves was a reality of the slave trade and life on American plantations. So some masters employed physical restraints and tortures, in some cases displaying almost unimaginable callousness and cruelty. Some unruly slaves were forced to wear metal or leather collars. Slaveholders could buy such contrivances not only from blacksmiths but also in general stores; and some people made them in their homes or shops and advertised them in the classified sections of newspapers. A 1756 ad in the *London Advertiser* read: "Silver padlocks for

Iron slave collars such as these from the late 1700s were used to control unruly slaves.

blacks or dogs,"[44] thereby equating slaves with animals. In fact, slaves who wore such collars were often held fast by ropes or chains in the very same manner as watchdogs and draft animals.

Collars were only one method used to restrain unruly slaves. Equiano recalled seeing masters hang heavy chains or iron hooks around their slaves' necks. These burdens were so heavy that the slaves were forced to stoop forward when they walked; moreover, it was impossible to run or fight while laden down with 60, 70, or 80 pounds (27, 32, or 36kg) of dead weight. Equiano also witnessed a fiendish device used widely in the Americas to punish or control unruly slaves. The young African was appalled at the treatment of a household slave

> who was cooking the dinner. And the poor creature was loaded with various kinds of iron machines. She had one particularly on her head, which locked her mouth so fast that she could scarcely speak; and could not eat nor drink. I was astonished and shocked at this contrivance, which I learned afterwards was called the iron muzzle.[45]

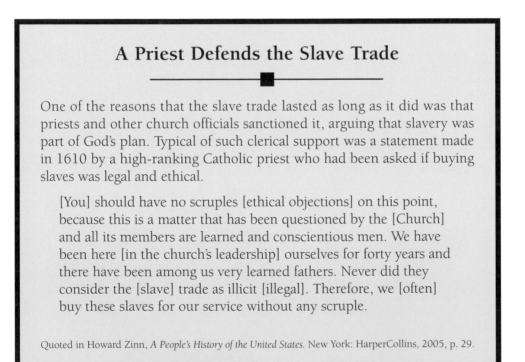

A Priest Defends the Slave Trade

One of the reasons that the slave trade lasted as long as it did was that priests and other church officials sanctioned it, arguing that slavery was part of God's plan. Typical of such clerical support was a statement made in 1610 by a high-ranking Catholic priest who had been asked if buying slaves was legal and ethical.

> [You] should have no scruples [ethical objections] on this point, because this is a matter that has been questioned by the [Church] and all its members are learned and conscientious men. We have been here [in the church's leadership] ourselves for forty years and there have been among us very learned fathers. Never did they consider the [slave] trade as illicit [illegal]. Therefore, we [often] buy these slaves for our service without any scruple.

Quoted in Howard Zinn, *A People's History of the United States*. New York: HarperCollins, 2005, p. 29.

Other common punishments and methods of control included branding with hot irons, slitting the nose, amputating a slave's ears or some toes and fingers, pulling out teeth, scalding with boiling water, and castrating male slaves. In addition, female slaves were often raped by their masters or their white overseers.

Besides physical restraints and gruesome punishments, there were also extensive laws designed to control the slaves. "If a [runaway] slave does not return," a Virginia law from the 1700s stated,

> anyone whatsoever may kill or destroy such slaves by such means as he shall think fit. . . . If the slave is apprehended [the law allows] such punishment for said slave either by dismembering, or in any other way [that the master involved] shall think fit . . . for the reclaiming [of] any such incorrigible [unruly] slave and terrifying others from the like practices. [46]

Fortunately, these inhumane methods and laws, coupled with the horrors of enslavement in Africa and the middle passage, were not destined to continue indefinitely. From the mid-1700s onward, they increasingly raised the ire of concerned citizens on both sides of the Atlantic. Once the abolitionist movement gained momentum, it was unstoppable. And the centuries-long subjugation and brutalization of untold millions of people could no longer endure.

Chapter Six

Abolition of the Slave Trade

Before about 1750, few people in Europe, or anywhere else on earth, argued that slavery was wrong. Even fewer called for the abolition of either the slave trade or slavery itself. The general view was that slavery was a natural part of the human condition. Spokesmen for the Catholic Church and other Christian denominations regularly cited passages from the Bible that clearly supported or sanctioned slavery. Among the most often quoted of these passages was one from the letters of St. Paul: "Tell slaves to be submissive to their masters and to give satisfaction in every respect. They are not to talk back, not to pilfer, but to show complete and perfect fidelity, so that in everything they may be an ornament to the doctrine of God our Savior."[47]

Other whites argued that the slave trade was necessary from a practical standpoint. How else, they asked, could plantation owners and other wealthy individuals expect to run large-scale, labor-intensive enterprises at a profit? Racism also played a role. Those who supported the slave trade sometimes admitted that enslaving other human beings might be wrong, but they insisted that African blacks were inferior to white people and not fully human, so enslaving them was not immoral. By and large, therefore, the slave trade and the use of slaves for labor was simply accepted by white Europeans and Americans as an expected, necessary, and justifiable fact of life.

This attitude began to change in the second half of the eighteenth century with the rise of the abolitionist movement. Abolitionist ideas took root first in Great Britain and France and then spread across the continent and the Atlantic. This new way of viewing slavery was, in the words of one modern historian, "a shift in moral consciousness" characterized by the "emergence of a widespread conviction that New World slavery symbolized all the forces that threatened the true destinies of man." The abolitionist movement thus "represented a momentous turning point in the evolution of man's moral perception." [48]

Influence of the Enlightenment

The great intellectual turning point that underpinned the abolitionist movement was the emergence of the European Enlightenment and the new ideas advocated by those who spearheaded it. The European Enlightenment was a movement of thinkers and writers who lived in the seventeenth and eighteenth centuries. Most of these individuals were British or French, but they influenced intellectuals in nations and colonies throughout Europe and the Americas. Enlightenment thinkers strongly supported religious freedom; the use of reason and science; fair government; and basic human rights, including freedom of speech and expression. According to Johannes Postma:

> Enlightenment advocates often encouraged social as well as political reform. Their ideal was to create a better world, making social injustice and exploitation targets for reform. Reformers called for improvement in the deplorable conditions in prisons and institutions for the mentally ill. Freedom, equality, and brotherhood became slogans for democratic revolutions that swept through Europe and the Americas. Some philosophers demanded equality for women. Several attacked slavery and the slave trade as inhumane. . . . This new intellectual environment encouraged anti-slavery sentiments. [49]

However, it soon became clear to abolitionists that outlawing slavery itself was going to be a long, difficult process. The institution

Jefferson Attacks the Slave Trade

It is not widely known today that when American founder Thomas Jefferson wrote the first draft of the Declaration of Independence, he included a clause calling for the abolition of the slave trade. Though he was himself a slave owner, as an Enlightenment thinker he viewed slavery as essentially immoral. Yet practically speaking, he realized that slavery was too entrenched, both socially and economically, to be removed all at once. So he opted for eliminating the slave trade first. His antislavery clause read in part:

> [The English king] has waged cruel war against human nature itself, violating its most sacred rights of life and liberty in the persons of a distant people [black Africans] who never offended him, captivating and carrying them into slavery in another hemisphere, or to incur miserable death in their transportation [across the Atlantic].

Shocked by this remarkable assault on the slave trade, delegates from several southern states, which were economically dependent on slavery, demanded that the clause be removed. And the United States lost its chance to lead the world in banning the slave trade.

Quoted in Carl Becker, *The Declaration of Independence: A Study in the History of Political Ideas.* New York: Harcourt, Brace, 1922, pp. 212–13.

of slavery was so deeply entrenched, both economically and socially, that no human government, even the most enlightened, was ready for what was then seen as a very drastic move. The fact that the founders of the infant United States, who advocated freedom and equality, did not immediately end slavery clearly illustrates this attitude. As a result, abolitionists instead adopted the strategy of accomplishing a more realistic goal first: abolishing the slave trade. Once that goal had been achieved, they reasoned, there would be a better chance of eliminating slavery itself.

Converting People One by One

The abolitionists therefore targeted the slave trade, denouncing the trafficking of human beings in an increasing flood of books, essays, newspaper articles, and public speeches. Abolitionists steadily won over ministers and other clergymen, who lectured their flocks about the evils of the trade. In this way, person by person, household by household, and congregation by congregation, people who had once taken slavery for granted were converted to the abolitionist cause.

A famous case of such conversion was that of John Newton (born 1725), a British ship captain who began as a commander

John Newton wrote the hymn *Amazing Grace* after converting to Christianity and abandoning his work in the slave trade.

of slave ships but in the 1750s joined the abolitionist movement. His change of heart and subsequent vehement opposition to the slave trade poignantly illustrate the deep hatred the abolitionists felt for the trade and their strong commitment to ending it. In one of the many public speeches he delivered against the trade, Newton declared:

> I hope it always will be a subject of humiliating reflection to me that I was once an active instrument in a business at which my heart now shudders. Perhaps what I have said of myself may be applicable to the nation at large. The slave trade was always unjustifiable. But inattention and disinterest prevented for a time the evil from being perceived. It is otherwise at present. The mischiefs and evils connected with it have been of late years represented with such undeniable evidence . . . that hardly an objection can be made to the almost universal wish for the suppression of this trade. [50]

Newton was even more passionate in his condemnation of the slave trade in the following remarks:

> There is a cry of blood against us—a cry accumulated by the accession of fresh victims, of thousands, of scores of thousands, of hundreds of thousands from year to year. . . . If the trade is at present carried on to the same extent and nearly in the same manner, while we are delaying from year to year to put a stop to our part in it, the blood of many thousands of our helpless, much injured fellow creatures is crying against us. The pitiable state of the survivors who are torn from their relatives, connections, and their native land must be taken into account. Enough of this horrid scene. I fear the African trade is a national sin. [51]

The Quakers and William Wilberforce

Newton was a Protestant who argued that God abhorred the slave trade. Other abolitionists used similar arguments. But no one was more influential in turning people of faith against the slave trade than the Society of Friends, better known as the Quakers. The Quakers, who believed in the spiritual equality of all humans, including slaves, were particularly numerous and vocal in Britain

A Slave Trader Becomes an Abolitionist

An English slave trader, John Newton, eventually gave up his role in the trade and became a prominent abolitionist. Quoted here are statements he later made about his conversion.

> During the time that I was engaged in the slave trade, I never had the least scruple as to its lawlessness. I was, on the whole, satisfied with it, [thinking of it] as the appointment Providence [God] had marked out for me. . . . I only thought myself bound to treat the slaves under my care with gentleness. [But I eventually saw that what I was doing was wrong.] I consider myself bound in conscience to bear my testimony at least and to wash my hands from the guilt [and] to take shame to myself by a public confession, which, however sincere, comes too late to prevent or repair the misery and mischief to which I have formerly been accessory.

Quoted in Thomas Howard, ed., *Black Voyage: Eyewitness Accounts of the Atlantic Slave Trade*. Boston: Little, Brown, 1971, pp. 206–8.

and colonial America. At first, a number of Quakers owned slaves and merely advocated treating them humanely. But by the late 1760s the Quakers were advocating the more radical idea of freeing all those presently in servitude. In a meeting held in Philadelphia in 1776, the year the British colonies became the United States, American Quaker leaders urged the church to excommunicate (expel) members who did not free their slaves.

The Quakers were also noteworthy for their pioneering work in eliminating the slave trade through political persuasion and new laws. Abolitionist organizations founded by Quakers gained adherents in Britain, France, and the United States in the 1780s. These groups produced and distributed pamphlets condemning the slave trade, organized boycotts against merchants who supported the trade, and urged politicians to introduce legislation banning the trade. Particularly influential was Thomas Clarkson (1760–1846). Though not a Quaker himself, he allied himself with leading Quakers and heavily lobbied members of Britain's Parliament to abolish the slave trade.

Among the legislators Clarkson worked with and influenced was William Wilberforce, an evangelical Christian who became a member of Parliament at age twenty in 1780. A vigorous opponent of the slave trade, Wilberforce became Britain's chief and most vocal abolitionist. His repeated efforts to ban the trade first resulted in the 1788 Dolben Act, which improved conditions aboard British slave ships. In 1792 Wilberforce and his supporters managed to pass an outright ban of the trade in one of Parliament's two houses, the House of Commons. However, the other house, the more conservative House of Lords, vetoed the bill. Still, it was now clear to all involved that the abolitionist movement would ultimately prevail.

Impact of Slave Rebellions

Meanwhile, abolitionists and their cause gained strength through the impact of increasing resistance and rebellions by slaves in the Americas. For decades, runaway slaves in various parts of the Caribbean and Central and South America had banded together with other escapees. They had formed secret societies, most often referred to as Maroons, that inhabited inaccessible wilderness areas. Members of these societies sometimes helped other slaves escape from plantations.

Even as Maroon societies grew larger in the late 1700s, large-scale slave uprisings became more and more common. In 1763 slaves launched an insurrection and nearly took over the Dutch colony of Guyana (on South America's northern coast). The biggest and most influential slave rebellion took place in the French colony of St. Domingue. Local Maroon communities regularly raided white-owned plantations there in the 1780s. Then, in August 1791, a very large Maroon-led uprising exploded in the northern sector of the colony. Its leader, Boukman Dutty, declared:

> The god who created the sun which gives us light, who rouses the waves and rules the storm . . . watches us. He sees all that the white man does. The god of the white man inspires him with crime, but our god calls upon us

to do good works. Our god . . . will direct our arms and aid us. . . . Listen to the voice of liberty, which speaks in the hearts of us all. [52]

The rebellion soon spread throughout the colony. Other black leaders rose from among the slaves, the most famous being Toussaint L'Ouverture and Jean-Jacques Dessalines. These men led the slaves in a number of military victories over the French. In 1803 St. Domingue became the independent nation of Haiti, with a government run by former slaves. This event had a huge impact on the slave trade because many wealthy merchants now feared that similar rebellions would become commonplace. That would make investing large sums of money in the trade much too

Toussaint L'Ouverture, a former slave, leads a rebellion against the French.

risky a venture. Increasingly, white slaveholders began to perceive that the potential financial losses of the slave trade might outweigh its potential financial gains.

The Slave Trade Banned

The success of the slaves in Haiti in 1803 galvanized the abolitionist movement, especially in Britain and the United States. The British Empire abolished the slave trade in all its territories by an

Samuel Crowther was one of thousands of slaves rescued and freed by British warships.

act of Parliament in 1807. Also in 1807, legislators in the United States, urged on by President Thomas Jefferson, passed a law forbidding further importation of slaves after January 1, 1808.

Parliament not only banned slave-trading by British merchants and ships, but also led the way in ending participation in the trade by other nations. At first, the British government used diplomacy to achieve this goal. At the Congress of Vienna in 1815, for instance, Great Britain convinced the French and Dutch to condemn and abolish the trade. Britain also persuaded Portugal and Spain to limit their slave ships to sea-lanes south of the equator beginning in 1817.

It was not long, however, before Britain resorted to more overt measures to stop the remaining slave trade. In 1819 the British created an anti–slave trade squadron of warships that began patrolling the Atlantic. These vessels hunted down and captured slave ships from other nations. At first reluctantly, France and the United States joined this effort. Slave traders now became the equivalent of international pirates. At least 160,000 slaves were rescued and freed as a result of this international campaign.

One of these freed slaves was a Nigerian named Ajaya, who after gaining his freedom took the name of Samuel Crowther. He had been captured at age thirteen in 1820. Taken to the coast in a slow journey of almost two years, he was sold to a Portuguese slaver and placed on a ship bound for Brazil. Ajaya was chained to several other African boys and men, who were forced to lie close together in a small room in the hold. "We were almost suffocated or bruised to death in a room with one door," Ajaya later recalled. "Very often at night, when two or three individuals quarreled or fought, the whole drove [group] suffered punishment without any distinction."[53]

Fortunately for Ajaya and his companions, a squadron of British vessels suddenly appeared and captured the slave ship and its owners. "In a few days we were quite at home on the [British] man-of war [*Myrmidon*]," Ajaya later wrote. "We were soon furnished with clothes. Our Portuguese owner and his son were brought over into the same vessel, bound in fetters, and thinking that I should no more get into his hand, I had the boldness to strike him on the head."[54] The British not only treated the captured slave trader harshly—by chaining, convicting, and imprisoning him—but also took his vessel completely out of commission. Ajaya remembered seeing the British sailors strip off the ship's rigging and abandon it at sea, its certain fate to sink into oblivion beneath the waves.

A Concerted and Noble Effort

Having succeeded in banning most of the slave trade, abolitionists now vigorously attacked the institution of slavery itself. The

---

William Wilberforce

William Wilberforce was the world's leading advocate of the abolition of the Atlantic slave trade in the late 1700s and early 1800s. Born into a wealthy British family, in his teens he was strongly influenced by abolitionist crusaders, especially former slave ship captain John Newton. Wilberforce decided to use his wealth and influence to destroy the trade. To this end he managed to become a member of Parliament when he was only twenty. He lobbied his fellow legislators incessantly to end the slave trade, introducing an abolition bill every year until it finally passed the House of Commons in 1792. Although the House of Lords vetoed the bill, Wilberforce refused to give up. The bill finally passed both houses of Parliament on May 1, 1807. Having achieved this great milestone, he then devoted himself untiringly to the abolition of the slavery institution itself, which Parliament approved in the 1830s. Wilberforce's heroic efforts against slavery are the subject of the 2007 movie *Amazing Grace,* directed by Michael Apted.

Briton William Wilberforce used his wealth and influence to help destroy the slave trade.

British Empire led the way again by banning slavery in all its territories and colonies worldwide in 1838. The United States, partly because of pressures created during its Civil War, abolished slavery in the 1860s. By that time, the only places in the Western Hemisphere that still allowed slavery were Brazil (which became independent of Portugal in 1822) and the Spanish colonies of Cuba and Puerto Rico. These final outposts of slavery gradually gave it up, Brazil being the last to do so in 1888.

Seen from a modern vantage, the abolition of the Atlantic slave trade was a long, concerted effort undertaken by thousands of individuals, private organizations, and national governments. The thinkers of the Enlightenment, the Quakers and other religious groups, heroic individuals such as Newton, Clarkson, and Wilberforce, and many others all played their parts. But no single force in this noble effort was as relentless as Great Britain once it set itself against the trade. Few today would argue with the words of the noted nineteenth-century Irish historian W.E.H. Lecky. "The unweary, unostentatious [straightforward], and inglorious [unglamorous] crusade of England against slavery," he said, "may probably be regarded as among the three or four perfectly virtuous pages comprised in the history of nations."[55]

The Slave Trade's Grim Legacy

Although the Atlantic slave trade was abolished and eliminated in the nineteenth century, its impact lingered and its effects can still be felt today in various parts of the world. First, the trade disrupted and corrupted many of the African societies that took part in it. As one modern scholar sums it up:

> Large numbers of [West Africa's] young men and women, most in the prime of their life, were carried off, never to return. Because the initial enslavement was largely carried out by Africans and orchestrated by men in leadership positions, the slave trade undermined the very foundation of traditional [African] political institutions and gave rise to warlords and new states that often concentrated their efforts on hunting people.[56]

The African warlords and slave hunters bred by the slave trade often became dependent on the revenues collected from white slave merchants. So there was a tendency for kings and chieftains to extend their slaving activities inland, bringing incessant war and mass kidnapping to areas that had long been relatively peaceful. This violence set one African society against another, leaving a legacy of distrust and intertribal rivalries that continued long after the slave trade ended.

Expanding Global Populations

Another direct effect the slave trade had on Africa, as well as on Europe and the Americas, was to significantly increase population growth over the course of two to three centuries. The main cause of this growth was the raising, by slave labor, of enormous quantities of certain staple food crops in the Americas and the spread of these staples to Europe and Africa. For example, corn, cassava, and sweet potatoes grown in the Americas were exported to Africa. There, these crops stimulated population growth even while the slave trade itself was depleting local populations; as a result, parts of West Africa managed to keep replenishing their populations despite the ravages of the trade. At the same time more than 50 million people emigrated from Europe to the Americas in the 1700s. Yet the population of Europe actually increased in this period.

Partly because of these population increases in Europe and the Americas, many nations in these regions expanded their territories. This was accomplished either through colonization (as in the case of England establishing colonies across the globe) or annexation of neighboring lands (as in the case of the United States absorbing Native American lands in its westward expansion to the Pacific coast). The subsequent economic, political, and military successes of these nations were therefore indirectly attributable to the inexpensive labor and huge-scale food production of millions of captive slaves. In the words of Herbert S. Klein, a leading scholar of the slave trade: "Without that [cheap African] labor, most of America would never have developed at the pace it did."[57]

Still an Open Wound

Today these economic, demographic, and political effects of the slave trade are known mainly to academics. Much more obvious to average people are the debilitating effects of the aftermath of the slave trade on the lives of generations of the descendants of black slaves. Slavery and the slave trade created a permanent underclass of people of African descent in the United States and other sectors of the Americas. From the mid-1800s to the mid-1900s, African Americans were free. Yet whites still deemed blacks inferior, and therefore African Americans experienced a great deal of racial prejudice, poverty, and social and political inequality.

Civil rights supporters march in front of the Lincoln Memorial in Washington, D.C., in 1963.

The civil rights movement that began in the United States in the 1950s eliminated some of these ills suffered by the descendants of slaves. However, both white and black leaders acknowledge that racism still exists in America. Moreover, experts on the slave trade point out that the long-lasting negative effects of the trade on the United States are not systematically taught in schools and therefore not widely known. As American historian Henry L. Gates stated in 2001:

Until we as a society fully reckon with the history of slavery in all its dimensions . . . and overcome our historical denial of the central shaping role that slavery has played in the creation of America's social, political, cultural, and economic institutions, we cannot truly begin to confront the so-called race problem in this country.[58]

This reluctance to acknowledge the full extent of the legacy of the slave trade can be seen in recent international diplomatic developments. In 2001 the World Conference Against Racism was held in Durban, South Africa. A majority of African countries attending the meeting demanded that the former slave-trading nations make public apologies for their roles in the trade. But the United States, the United Kingdom, Spain, Portugal, and the Netherlands refused. Experts speculate that these countries feared that an apology might open the door to demands that they pay monetary compensation to the descendants of slaves. In November 2006 Tony Blair, the British prime minister, offered a partial apology for his country's role in the slave trade. However, a number of African leaders dismissed his words as too casual and too late to repair past damages. These incidents demonstrate that one of history's most horrendous holocausts remains in a sense an open wound on the psyche of former slaves and former slave traders alike.

Notes

Introduction: Considering the African Perspective

1. "The Maafa: A Holocaust of Greed." www.geocities.com/CollegePark/Classroom/9912/maafa.html.

2. African Holocaust, "Transatlantic Slavery (Maafa)." www.africanholocaust.net/articles/TRANSATLANTIC%20SLAVE%20TRADE.htm.

3. Kwaku Person-Lynn, "African Involvement in the Atlantic Slave Trade." www.africawithin.com/kwaku/afrikan_involvement.htm.

4. Person-Lynn, "African Involvement in the Atlantic Slave Trade."

5. Anne C. Bailey, *African Voices of the Atlantic Slave Trade*. Boston: Beacon, 2006, p. 227.

6. Maulana Karenga, "The Ethics of Reparations: Engaging the Holocaust of Enslavement." www.africawithin.com/karenga/ethics.htm.

7. Bailey, *African Voices*, pp. 230–31.

Chapter One: The Rise of the Slave Trade

8. Thomas Howard, ed., *Black Voyage: Eyewitness Accounts of the Atlantic Slave Trade*. Boston: Little, Brown, 1971, p. 5.

9. Stuart B. Schwartz, *Slaves, Peasants, and Rebels: Reconsidering Brazilian Slavery*. Urbana: University of Illinois Press, 1996, p. 40.

10. Johannes Postma, *The Atlantic Slave Trade*. Westport, CT: Greenwood, 2005, p. 10.

11. Madeleine Burnside and Rosemarie Robotham, *Spirit of the Passage: The Transatlantic Slave Trade in the Seventeenth Century*. New York: Simon & Schuster, 1997, p. 64.

Chapter Two: Slavery Comes to Colonial America

12. Howard Zinn, *A People's History of the United States*. New York: HarperCollins, 2005, p. 25.

13. Quoted in Zinn, *People's History*, p. 25.

14. Ulrich B. Phillips, *American Negro Slavery*. Whitefish, MT: Kessenger, 2004, p. 77.

15. Quoted in Hugh Thomas, *The Slave Trade: The Story of the Atlantic Slave Trade, 1440–1870*. New York: Simon & Schuster, 1997, p. 431.

16. Quoted in Zinn, *People's History*, p. 31.

17. Burnside and Robotham, *Spirit of the Passage*, p. 62.

Chapter Three: Acquiring Slaves in Africa

18. Quoted in Zinn, *People's History,* p. 27.

19. Quoted in Howard, *Black Voyage,* p. 38.

20. Burnside and Robotham, *Spirit of the Passage,* p. 86.

21. Quoted in Paul Edwards, ed., *Equiano's Travels.* Oxford: Harcourt, 1996, pp. 13–14.

22. Quoted in Elizabeth Donnan, ed., *Documents Illustrative of the Slave Trade to America,* vol. 2. Washington, DC: Carnegie Institution, 1935, p. 635.

23. Quoted in Donnan, *Documents Illustrative of the Slave Trade,* p. 634.

24. Quoted in Donnan, *Documents Illustrative of the Slave Trade,* p. 640.

25. Quoted in P.E.H. Hair et al., eds., *Barbot on Guinea.* London: Hakluyt Society, 1992, p. 493.

26. Quoted in Hair, *Barbot on Guinea,* p. 392.

27. Burnside and Robotham, *Spirit of the Passage,* p. 105.

Chapter Four: The Dreaded Middle Passage

28. Quoted in Kenneth F. Kipple, *The Caribbean Slave Trade: A Biological History.* New York: Cambridge University Press, 1985, p. 57.

29. Willem Bosman, *A New and Accurate Description of the Coast of Guinea.* London: Frank Cass, 1967, p. 364.

30. Quoted in Edwards, *Equiano's Travels,* p. 24.

31. Quoted in Zinn, *People's History,* p. 28.

32. Quoted in Edwards, *Equiano's Travels,* p. 25.

33. Quoted in Edwards, *Equiano's Travels,* p. 26.

34. Bosman, *New and Accurate Description,* p. 365.

35. Quoted in George F. Dow, *Slave Ships and Slavery.* Brattleboro, VT: Marine Research Society, 1927, p. 27.

36. Postma, *Atlantic Slave Trade,* p. 45.

37. Quoted in Howard, *Black Voyage,* p. 51.

Chapter Five: Final Destinations of the Enslaved

38. Burnside and Robotham, *Spirit of the Passage,* p. 12.

39. Quoted in Edwards, *Equiano's Travels,* p. 28.

40. Postma, *Atlantic Slave Trade,* pp. 30–31.

41. Quoted in Edwards, *Equiano's Travels,* p. 29.

42. Quoted in Howard, *Black Voyage,* p. 112.

43. Quoted in Edwards, *Equiano's Travels,* pp. 30–31.

44. Quoted in Bailey, *African Voices*, p. 142.

45. Quoted in Arna Bontemps, ed., *Great Slave Narratives*. Boston: Beacon, 1969, p. 76.

46. Quoted in Zinn, *People's History*, p. 34.

Chapter Six: Abolition of the Slave Trade

47. Titus 2:9–10.

48. David B. Davis, *The Problem of Slavery in Western Culture*. Ithaca, NY: Cornell University Press, 1966, p. 42.

49. Postma, *Atlantic Slave Trade,* p. 64.

50. Quoted in Howard, *Black Voyage,* p. 208.

51. Quoted in Howard, *Black Voyage,* p. 209.

52. Quoted in Colin Waugh, "The Haitian Revolution and Atlantic Slavery."

http://archive.workersliberty.org/wlmags/wl102/haiti.htm.

53. Quoted in Philip D. Curtain, ed., *Africa Remembered: Narratives by West Africans from the Era of the Slave Trade*. Prospect Heights, IL: Waveland, 1997, p. 314.

54. Quoted in Curtain, *Africa Remembered,* pp. 315–16.

55. Quoted in Thomas, *Slave Trade,* p. 798.

Epilogue: The Slave Trade's Grim Legacy

56. Postma, *Atlantic Slave Trade,* p. 58.

57. Herbert S. Klein, *The Atlantic Slave Trade*. New York: Cambridge University Press, 1999, p. 102.

58. Quoted in Postma, *Atlantic Slave Trade,* p. 83.

Chronology

1444

The Portuguese transport 240 black slaves from West Africa to Lisbon.

1492

Sailing for Spain, Italian explorer Christopher Columbus lands in what is now the Caribbean, initiating a European rush to exploit the Americas.

1494

In the Treaty of Tordesillas, Spain and Portugal divide up the Atlantic sphere into two general regions, each controlled by one of the signatories.

1538

The first black African slaves arrive in Brazil, which quickly becomes the largest plantation colony in the Americas.

1607

English settlers land in Jamestown, in what becomes the colony of Virginia.

1619

Twenty black slaves arrive in Virginia, the first Africans shipped to the English North American colonies.

1627

England establishes its first sugar plantation on the island of Barbados.

1740

Crew members kill 213 African slaves during an uprising aboard a Dutch slave ship.

1776

The colonists in Great Britain's thirteen North American colonies declare their independence, thereby creating the United States.

1781

The captain of a British slave ship throws 133 slaves overboard, igniting loud protests by abolitionists.

1801–1809

Years of the presidency of Thomas Jefferson, who lobbies hard for the abolition of the slave trade.

1807

Britain becomes the first nation to ban the slave trade.

1808

The United States abolishes the slave trade, although slavery itself remains legal.

1819

Great Britain creates an antislavery squadron of warships that begin intercepting slave ships in the Atlantic.

1838

The British Empire abolishes slavery in all its colonies around the world.

1865

The Thirteenth Amendment to the Constitution bans slavery in the United States.

1888

Brazil becomes the last country in the Americas to abolish slavery.

For Further Information

Books

Anne C. Bailey, *African Voices of the Atlantic Slave Trade*. Boston: Beacon, 2006. A descendant of black slaves attempts to examine the Atlantic slave trade through African sources, some of them only recently discovered.

Nigel Bolland, *Struggles for Freedom: Essays on Slavery, Colonialism, and Culture in the Caribbean and Central America*. Belize: Angelus, 1997. A collection of essays, each by an expert, exploring various aspects of the transatlantic slave trade.

Madeleine Burnside and Rosemarie Robotham, *Spirit of the Passage: The Transatlantic Slave Trade in the Seventeenth Century*. New York: Simon & Schuster, 1997. A well-researched and easy-to-read synopsis of the slave trade and how it affected both white and black societies in the seventeenth century.

Basil Davidson, ed., *African Civilization Revisited*. Trenton, NJ: Africa World Press, 1991. Tells about the role played by Africans in the slave trade and how the trade affected African societies.

Thomas Howard, ed., *Black Voyage: Eyewitness Accounts of the Atlantic Slave Trade*. Boston: Little, Brown, 1971.

One of the best available collections of eyewitness descriptions of the slave trade. Highly recommended.

Johannes Postma, *The Atlantic Slave Trade*. Westport, CT: Greenwood, 2005. An excellent overview of the slave trade, with many revealing statistics about the numbers of slaves shipped from Africa to the Americas.

Jonathan T. Reynolds and Erik Gilbert, *Africa in World History*. New York: Prentice Hall, 2003. An easy-to-read overview of African history, including the slave trade and European colonial policy in the area.

William St. Clair, *The Door of No Return: The History of Cape Coast Castle and the Atlantic Slave Trade*. New York: Bluebridge, 2007. An examination of one of the most famous European strongholds and slave emporiums on the shores of western Africa.

Internet Sources

The Afrocentric Experience, "The Maafa (African Holocaust)." www.swagga.com/maafa.htm. Contains several links to articles about the Atlantic slave trade, mostly by black writers.

The Terrible Transformation, "Virginia's Slave Codes." www.pbs.org/wgbh/aia/part1/1p268.html. Describes several of the laws passed in colonial Virginia to control the blacks brought to the colony by slave traders.

Colin Waugh, "The Haitian Revolution and Atlantic Slavery." http://archive.workersliberty.org/wlmags/wl102/haiti.htm. An informative overview of the slave uprisings in Haiti that contributed to the eventual abolition of the Atlantic slave trade.

Wilberforce Central.org, "Tribute to William Wilberforce." www.wilberforcecentral.org/wfc/Wilberforce/index.htm. An excellent brief overview of the key figure in the abolition of the slave trade, with links to related topics.

Index

Picture Credits

Cover: © CORBIS

AP Images, 86

The Art Archive/Bibliothéque des Arts Décoratifs, Paris/Gianni Dagli Orti, 22

The Art Archive/Maarine Museum, Lisbon/Gianni Dagli Orti, 20

The Art Archive/Musee des Arts Africains Océaniens/Gianni Dagli Orti, 44

HIP/Art Resource, N.Y., 11, 15, 42

Snark/Art Resource, N.Y., 34

© Private Collection/The Bridgeman Art Library, 53

© Private Collection/© Michael Graham-Stewart/The Bridgeman Art Library, 69

© Private Collection/Peter Newark American Pictures/The Bridgeman Art Library, 60

© Wilburforce House, Hull City Museums and Art Galleries, U.K./The Bridgeman Art Library, 82

© Bettmann/CORBIS, 51, 56, 79

© Stapleton Collection/CORBIS, 80

The Gale Group, 25

Hulton Archive/Getty Images, 17, 27, 29, 31, 46

Time & Life Pictures/Getty Images, 12, 40

Mike Simons/Getty Images, 64

© Fotomas/TopFoto/The Image Works, 75

The Library of Congress, 35, 47

© North Wind/North Wind Picture Archives, 33

About the Author

In addition to his acclaimed volumes on the ancient world, historian Don Nardo has written and edited many books for young adults about modern European and American history, including *The Age of Colonialism, The French Revolution, The Mexican-American War, The Declaration of Independence, The Bill of Rights,* and *The Great Depression.* Mr. Nardo also writes screenplays and teleplays and composes music. He lives with his wife, Christine, in Massachusetts.